A Workbook for Healing

Adult Children of Alcoholics

Patty McConnell

PERENNIAL LIBRARY

Harper & Row, Publishers, San Francisco
Cambridge, Hagerstown, New York, Philadelphia, Washington
London, Mexico City, São Paulo, Singapore, Sydney

To my husband and daughters

The author gratefully acknowledges the permission to reprint material from the following works. *The Experience of Insight: A Simple and Direct Guide to Buddhist Meditation*, copyright © 1983 by Joseph Goldstein. Reprinted by permission of Shambhala Publications, Inc. *Handbook to Higher Consciousness*, by Ken Keyes, Jr. Copyright © 1975 by Living Love Publishers. Reprinted with permission. *The Hiding Place*, by Corrie ten Boom with John and Elizabeth Sherrill. Reprinted by permission of Chosen Books, Inc., Chappaqua, New York. *Love is Leting Go of Fear*, copyright © 1979 by Gerald G. Jampolsky. Reprinted with permission. *Positive Therapy: Making the Best of Everything*, copyright © 1977 by Allen E. Wiesen. Reprinted with permission. *The Song of the Bird*, copyright © 1982 by Anthony de Mello, S.J. Reprinted by permission of Doubleday and Company, Inc. *Your Inner Child of the Past*, copyright © 1963 by W. Hugh Missildine. Reprinted with permission. *The Way of Chuang Tzu*, by Thomas Merton. Copyright © 1965 by the Abbey Gethsemani. Reprinted by permission of New Directions Publishing Corp.

Library of Congress Cataloging in Publication Data

McConnell, Patty.
  A workbook for healing. (Previously published under title Adult children of alcoholics.)

  Bibliography: p. 168.
  1. Alcoholics—United States—Family relationships.
2. Adult children—United States—Family relationships.
3. Self-perception. I. Title.
HV5132.M38 1986   362.2'92   86-14898
ISBN 0-86683-526-1

87 88 89 90 10 9 8 7 6 5

Contents

The Golden Eagle

A man found an eagle's egg and put it in the nest of a backyard hen. The eaglet hatched with the brood of chicks and grew up with them.

All his life the eagle did what the backyard chickens did, thinking he was a backyard chicken. He scratched the earth for worms and insects. He clucked and cackled. And he would thrash his wings and fly a few feet into the air like the chickens. After all, that is how a chicken is supposed to fly, isn't it?

Years passed and the eagle grew very old. One day he saw a magnificent bird far above him in the cloudless sky. It floated in graceful majesty among the powerful wind currents, with scarcely a beat of its strong golden wings.

The old eagle looked up in awe. "Who's that?" he said to his neighbour.

"That's the eagle, the king of the birds," said his neighbour. "But don't give it another thought. You and I are different from him."

So the eagle never gave it another thought. He died thinking he was a backyard chicken.

—Anthony de Mello,
The Song of the Bird

Preface

There is a Zen story I'd like to share.

> Two monks were returning home in the evening to their
> temple. It had been raining and the road was very muddy.
> They came to an intersection where a beautiful girl was
> standing, unable to cross the street because of the mud. Just
> in the moment, the first monk picked her up in his arms and
> carried her across. The monks then continued on their way.
> Later that night the second monk, unable to restrain himself
> any longer, said to the first, "How could you do that?! We
> monks should not even look at females, much less touch
> them. Especially young and beautiful ones." "I left the girl
> there," the first monk said, "are you still carrying her?"[1]

What are you "still carrying"? Guilt? Anger? I wrote this workbook to
help you identify what you need to leave on the road. I know how
important this is, for I too am the child of an alcoholic.

My personal healing process began in the spring of 1980. At that time,
with my life out of balance and my spirit in depression, I made the decision
to get well. But wellness terrified me, for I knew I had to face who I was
without depending on my familiar escapes: alcohol, tranquilizers, overeating.
I created most of the exercises in this workbook to help me find peace
during that first year and to gain insight during the years that followed.
The therapists who guided my writing of this book suggested other
exercises; still others came from fellow adult children of alcoholics, fellow
pilgrims.

As one of those pilgrims recently said to me, "I want to get well so I can
love other people. But before I can love others, I have to love myself. And
before I can love myself, I have to discover who I am."

And so I offer you this "workbook for healing." It is a process of self-
discovery, a way to realize what needs to be left on the road, a journey to
freedom.

Introduction

"Why don't I trust anyone?" asked Bill. "Why am I always afraid? At work. At my own dinner table."

Bill is an adult child of an alcoholic. He is not alone. Research indicates that over twenty-two million adult Americans grew up in homes where one parent, or both, were alcoholic. Today millions of adults suffer as Bill suffers. I know. I too am the child of an alcoholic.

Our physical disorders can devitalize us: headaches, hypertension, stomach and digestive tract disorders. Our dysfunctions can demoralize us: many failed relationships, eating compulsions, alcoholism. As a physician said: "I believe adult children of alcoholics comprise one of the largest unrecognized, unhealed segments of the American population."

How did all this happen? In innocence, you and I made decisions out of our need to stabilize tumultuous early home lives. We must be proud of ourselves; our decisions kept us alive. But in adulthood many of those decisions promote chaos. Today is a composite of what was and what is, a composite of confusion.

This workbook untangles that confusion by inviting you, an adult child of an alcoholic, to restructure past decisions. The book asks you to reexamine childhood experiences with an adult awareness. In Part I, "The Hurt," you will return to your early environment. You will examine what took place there: the beliefs you established, the roles you took on, and the ways you may have sabotaged your sincere efforts to grow. In Part II, "The Healing," you can modify your feelings and defenses, and change the past and present behaviors they have encouraged, as you evolve on your way towards wholeness. The exercises in the book were endorsed by therapists for those purposes.

Before you begin, understand that healing is neither immediate nor linear. You don't start at point A (pain) and rush to point B (recovery) in a straight line. You need time to travel up one day, down a little the next, and perhaps up again the third. Healing occurs as you walk hills and meadows. Be patient and gentle with yourself on your journey.

If you're frightened by the amount or depth of material in the book, again, be patient and gentle. You may decide to use the workbook only once a week or for short periods of time. Better to get well in small steps than to throw out a chance for recovery because the process appears weighty. A timing device might help you. Set the oven timer for twenty minutes, work until the buzzer goes off, and then put the workbook away. Others have found that this practice diminishes fear. Respecting your limits and setting guidelines will keep the material manageable.

Using affirmations is another way to protect yourself and keep the material manageable. Affirmations are positive statements that you declare to be true. "I am lovable," for example, or "I allow only good to fill my life." When you repeat positive statements, you envelop yourself in healing images and feelings and release yourself from negative directions. To help you, I have included an affirmation at the beginning of each chapter. It is there for peace and strength. I invite you to return again and again to a chapter's affirmation as you do that chapter's work.

When you work, you will discover that some of the conditions presented in the book don't apply to you. Description is not prescription. Isolate what does apply and tailor an individual recovery program. Do the work surrounding your particular problems. Buy new pencils and commit yourself to the process. Do the drawing, the charting, the creative exploring. This is your process; only you can effect a change, a healing. Only you can rewalk the journey and rename the landmarks.

After you have completed the journey, perhaps you'll crinkle your brow and say, "I didn't need a workbook. I knew that stuff all along." If that happens, smile. Of course you know the material. Adult children of alcoholics are experienced survivors. You developed powerful coping mechanisms as a child. The workbook is an instrument to help surface and channel those mechanisms for recovery.

Keeping a journal in conjunction with the workbook can enhance the process of recovery. A journal is a written record of the deepest self, what you think and what you feel; it invites daily contact with who you are and what is steeping within you. Nothing is judged, and nothing is critiqued. Not judging may feel awkward in the beginning, for self-judgment is a trait adult children have practiced for years. Perhaps, then, a journal is the place to initiate self-acceptance. Find a notebook and start to write down what you feel. If you like, you may record quotations you come upon or fantasies you experience. If your dreams become an important healing tool, as mine have (the idea for this book originated in a dream), you may decide to keep a dream diary, a separate receptacle for dreams and their interpretations. However you choose to proceed, with a journal, with a dream diary, or solely with the workbook, trust the part of you that knows what you need to do in order to get well.

The workbook effects recovery in various situations. First, you may use it for self-healing, reading the sections and completing the individual exercises. Second, you may wish to use the book in conjunction with

4

personal therapy. The book is also helpful in Adult Children of Alcoholics discussion groups.

No matter where you use the workbook, you need to make a contract before you begin. *No one will be blamed.* In life, people live the best they can with the information they have at the time. You did that. Your parents did that. Next time you point a finger at someone, notice that three fingers point back at you. Adult children cannot fault those who were unaware or ill. I have no right to judge anyone.

AS I PURSUE MY HEALING PROCESS,
I WILL BLAME NO ONE FOR WHAT HAPPENED,
OR IS HAPPENING, IN MY LIFE

Signature: _____

Date: _____

Follow the workbook at your own pace and be in touch with your individual needs. If any of the exercises create discomfort, understand that you can put them aside until you are ready. The workbook is flexible. You may disregard or return to exercises as you wish. Your healing process is a personal process. If you experience excessive anxiety at any point in the process, seek professional counseling. Your inner healing center knows what is best for you and will signal if something further is required. Trust yourself and your inherent wisdom.

With the contract made, your process has begun. I respect your determination and courage. A decision to change is hard to make, but it is the first step towards recovery. Although affected by the past, you have chosen to be a victim of it no longer. I respect your dignity.

May you find peace on your journey home to yourself.

Part I

The Hurt

Eye of night, weep a star for us.
— The Author

Chapter 1

A Decision to Change

I think, speak, and act
only health and wholeness in my life.

Set aside a period of time when you'll be uninterrupted, perhaps ten or fifteen minutes. During that period, you will be invited to relax and discover the room of your authentic self. The room is a safe harbor, a secure place that holds the answers to whatever you need to know. Once you experience the room, you may return there anytime you desire peace or knowledge.

EXERCISE #1

The Room of Your Authentic Self[1]

To begin, find a comfortable chair. When you are settled, close your eyes, take a deep breath, and say to yourself, *I breathe in eternal peace.* Hold the breath for a moment and then exhale, saying, *I breathe out eternal peace.* Repeat this procedure substituting the phrases "eternal harmony" and "eternal love."

Concentrate on your breathing. The breath in, the breath out. Begin to relax your body. Starting with your toes, say to yourself, *My toes are going to* relax, they are relaxing, they are relaxed. Move to your feet. Say, My feet are going to relax, they are relaxing, they are relaxed. Relax your ankles, then your calves, and slowly move up the rest of your body, relaxing each part, ending with your scalp.

You are now feeling peaceful. As you experience this pleasant state, let your mind float until it comes to a cozy room. Walk inside the room and gently shut the door. Feel the carpeting beneath your feet, the carpet's depth and texture. Breathe the freshness of the air. Notice how safe you feel here. You are aware that you have entered a sacred place. Let your internal eyes wander the room. The room is decorated with your favorite furniture and treasures. How secure you feel. Breathe in the security. Look out your window. The peacefulness of the scenery fills your being and instills a sense of unity. Breathe and relax. You are safe here. No one can intrude. All problems have healthy solutions in your room. Breathe and thank yourself for finding this peaceful sanctuary. You know you can return here anytime you wish, anytime you want to feel calm or secure. If a problem needs a healthy solution, you can come to this room for the answer. Your room is the home of your authentic self, the self you knew existed but didn't know how to find.

Take time to enjoy your special place. When you are ready, you will return to the present, understanding that, although you are an adult child of an alcoholic, you can make changes. You have found a room that can help you get well. Sense the peace in your awareness.

Take another moment. Open your eyes feeling secure and refreshed. You are an adult child of an alcoholic. You are healing.

GROWING UP IN AN ALCOHOLIC HOME

If you grew up in a home with an alcoholic parent, you grew up in confusion. Alcohol saw to that. Alcohol, however, did not decide how you perceived that confusion. You engineered the perceptions. You also devised defense mechanisms in order to live with those perceptions.

The defense mechanisms you created were powerful resources that kept you alive, but now those resources threaten your adult stability: they stop you from achieving your potential. They siphon off energy you could use for growth. Early coping mechanisms can blister adult relationships, parenting skills, and career advancement.

Childhood defense mechanisms are the number one reason adult children of alcoholics encounter emotional distress in their mid-twenties. After absorbing this realization, you may want to pitch each defense and distress into the trash. But don't. Everything you do and feel is important (including distresses and defenses). Everything you do and feel makes up who you are—and you are important.

Therefore, your experiences deserve respect. Anxiety, headaches, and ulcers are ways to get your attention. Behaviors that produce these symptoms are keys to unlock your unmet needs.

You begin to heal when you value all that you are. Once you respect your symptoms and behaviors, you can get under them to heal the emotional deprivation they represent. And emotional deprivations abound in adult children of alcoholics. The behaviors you implemented to ease those deprivations often retard adult growth. They are too much for the present time; they have been "overdeveloped."

The results of those overdeveloped defense mechanisms follow. Review the items listed. Take your time. Relax. As you examine them, ask yourself: Have I experienced the fear of abandonment? Have I experienced intimacy difficulties? And so forth. You will find you relate to some and not to others. Don't feel guilty if you haven't experienced everything on the list. No gold stars will be given for "biggest and baddest" behaviors. You may also find a few of your disorders are excluded. Simply add them.

- fear of abandonment
- intimacy difficulties
- distrust
- intenseness
- mood swings
- low self-esteem
- bulimia, anorexia nervosa, or overeating
- alcoholism, or alcoholism in a significant other
- lying
- excitement addiction
- dependency
- casual sex or other sexual disorders
- violent behavior, or violent behavior in a significant other
- excessive over- or underresponsibility
- excessive over- or underreaction
- impulsiveness
- critical judging
- inability to relax
- need to control
- need for approval
- compulsive behavior, or compulsive behavior in a significant other

EXERCISE #2

Part 1

Using examples from the list above, or examples of your own, write down the behaviors you feel cause problems in your life today. After you've done that, go back and number the behaviors from (1), the most troublesome, to (15), the least troublesome.

Part 2

Next, record the effects of the behaviors in your life. Not every effect is negative. Behaviors produce negatives and positives.

Example
Let's examine my impulsiveness.
Negative: *My impulsiveness costs me money. My sister lives hundreds of miles from me, yet I telephone her when I think of her, not when long distance rates are cheaper.*
Positive: *My impulsiveness helps me work with feelings in the "here and now." When I miss my sister, and talk to her about my sadness, I deal with the feeling immediately.*

If you sense discomfort working the assignment, you have choices. You can postpone the assignment and proceed to another section. You can take out your journal and write about the discomfort. You can accept the discomfort as a sign that you're getting better, like having achy muscles when you begin to exercise. You can go for a long walk. You can talk the discomfort through with a friend. You can return to the room of your authentic self for peace and direction. With this exercise, as with future exercises, you know what is best for you: use your power of choice. Respect yourself and follow what you know.

Behavior	Positive	Negative

1. _____

2. _____

3. _____

Behavior	Positive	Negative

4. _____

5. _____

6. _____

7. _____

8. _____

9. _____

Behavior	Positive	Negative

10. _____

11. _____

12. _____

13. _____

14. _____

15. _____

Part 3

Next, address each behavior by posing three questions:

A. How did you protect me as a child?

B. In what ways are you upsetting my adult life?

C. How can I help you become a balanced, productive behavior?
After asking each question, record the answer each behavior offers.
Answers to your problems are already within you. You only have to listen.
Address each behavior as a friend. After you ask your friend a question,
wait for the answer. You will hear it in your head in your own voice.

Example

A. Impulsive behavior, how did you protect me as a child?
My impulsiveness answered: *I taught you to think quickly
so you could anticipate problems before being criticized.*

B. Impulsive behavior, in what ways are you upsetting my
adult life? In response, my impulsiveness answered:
*When I make you jump into action without thinking, you solve
problems less effectively and then tell yourself you're dumb or
bad.*

C. Impulsive behavior, how can I help you become a
balanced, productive behavior in my life? In response,
my impulsiveness answered: *Don't act until you've checked
out your assumptions, and until I offer you two or three
creative solutions to a problem. Then follow the solution that is
most loving to you and others.*

Your response

A. How did you protect me as a child?

Behavior   **Answer**

1. _____

Behavior   **Answer**

2. _____

3. _____

4. _____

5. _____

6. _____

7. _____

8. _____

Behavior   **Answer**

9. _____

10. _____

11. _____

12. _____

13. _____

14. _____

15. _____

B. In what ways are you upsetting my adult life?

Behavior   **Answer**

1. _____

2. _____

3. _____

4. _____

5. _____

6. _____

7. _____

Behavior   **Answer**

8. _____

9. _____

10. _____

11. _____

12. _____

13. _____

14. _____

15. _____

C. How can I help you become a balanced, productive behavior?

Behavior   **Answer**

1. _____

2. _____

3. _____

4. _____

5. _____

6. _____

7. _____

Behavior   **Answer**

8. _____

9. _____

10. _____

11. _____

12. _____

13. _____

14. _____

15. _____

HEALING IS CHANGE

To live is to be in process. And the process? Becoming. The earth, Aunt Martha's crab apple tree, the pet spaniel, and even Aunt Martha are all in process. Everything in life evolves towards its purpose. Your healing is a part of your evolutionary process, a striving towards your potential or the fullness of who you can be.

You are using the workbook to identify problem behaviors and to make changes to effect recovery. You identified your behaviors in the previous exercises. Next you will address change.

Change is achieved by commitment to change, not just consent. I may agree I should think before acting or that I should stop smoking, but I won't do either until I commit to do the work. As Tony, an adult child, said: "Recognizing I'm an adult child of an alcoholic is the easy part. Doing something about it is another thing."

In *Positive Therapy: Making the Best of Everything*, Allen Wiesen, a clinical psychologist, encapsules the process of change this way:

> The will to change is nourished by the realization that
> change is not merely possible, but probable, if "one" is
> willing to expend the psychological energy that is necessary
> for change. Change means effort, conscious willing effort to
> be other than what we have been, to attain objectives of
> genuine meaning in our lives.[1]

Change demands intense work, so people usually don't change unless they hurt. When you're "sick and tired of being sick and tired," you'll act and make changes. Until then, you won't. You'll stick with familiar behavioral patterns, suffering the consequences, until the consequences are more painful than the effort to change.

A young Indian boy went to the village shaman. The boy was troubled and said to the elder, "Help me. There is a war inside my heart. Part of me wants to travel east, and another part wants to travel west. What do I do?"

The old man nodded. The boy's problem was a familiar one. "Within each man," the shaman said, "lives two dogs. Both dogs are strong and fight for the man's heart; one to go east, and one to go west. The man chooses which dog will win by deciding which dog he will feed."

The decision to change or not to change is yours. Which dog will you feed?

EXERCISE #3

Please give serious consideration to each question before you respond.

1. Am I willing to change?

2. Am I willing to do the work to change?

3. Am I willing to experience the pain that accompanies change?

If you made a decision to change by responding yes to the three questions, continue.

4. I will make the following changes in my life:

    Example
    Concerning my impulsiveness I wrote this:
    I will write my sister letters, and I will try to call her after five o'clock, when telephone rates are lower.

Your changes

Congratulate yourself. Send yourself flowers. You are making a significant leap in the recovery process. You are identifying problem behaviors resulting from early defense mechanisms, and you are choosing to balance and integrate them. Use the remainder of the workbook to carry out your decision. The workbook will help you examine the setting that necessitated those coping mechanisms. After you reexperience the setting, you can apply adult wisdom to your childhood perceptions to activate powerful changes.

Without action, your decision to change is hollow. Decision is the body. Action is the soul. You have decided to get well, to become more than you have been up to this time. With positive action, you will succeed.

Allen Wiesen offers the same message when he writes that "awareness without positive action leaves one's hands clean, but people hungry. Positive action, however, is the process through which one creates his own destiny. The present is the father of the future."[2]

When you are ready to go on, turn the page and begin your future by relooking at the past. Using positive action, walk forward without judgment or self-pity. Proceed slowly and be gentle with yourself.

Chapter 2

Background

I am empty of fear and guilt.
I am filled with acceptance and love.

In the words of Kathryn, an adult child of an alcoholic: "I remember 'hiding' in my room under the pretext of studying. Every night Dad yelled at someone, and every night I was afraid 'tonight' would be my turn. The ax would always fall, but we kids never knew which one of us would get it. I would listen to my Dad's footsteps, wondering if they were coming towards my door."

Growing up is difficult. Growing up in an alcoholic home can be devastating. "When I was about twelve, I decided no one could be trusted," Angela said. "Many times I'd tell Mother things, then the next night after a few drinks, she'd whip everything back at me distorted and ugly. I'd look to my father for help, but he'd shake his head, throw his arms into the air, and leave the room."

Millions of adults grew up in homes controlled by alcohol. Millions of children presently "live" in them. In the average American neighborhood, amidst porch swings and tricycles, every sixth house contains an alcoholic. Every fourth child in the classroom copes with nightmares similar to Kathryn's and Angela's.

THE ALCOHOLIC FAMILY SYSTEM

Writing about all people, in his book *Your Inner Child of the Past*, W. Hugh Missildine, M.D., has said:

> While the circumstances and relationships of our early years
> may not have been entirely comfortable, we learned about
> life and the world at large in this special childhood setting.
> We learned to adjust ourselves to this special emotional
> atmosphere and to call it "reality."[1]

Adult children of alcoholics grew up in an environment of madness. "Reality" was, and continues to be, chaos. Granted, no family is perfect; all families cross established borders upon occasion. But in alcoholic families, the parents and parameters are disabled. These families contain good people controlled by a destructive chemical, alcohol, which dictates what is possible and what happens. And what happens is chaotic.

As Dr. Missildine has emphasized, "A child develops his sense of being a worthwhile, capable, important and unique individual from the attention given him by his parents."[2] The attention adult children of alcoholics received from their parents was contaminated.

Mistakes

Healthy family structures permit mistakes and foster independent growth. Members are encouraged to explore life, to deepen themselves, and to take responsibility for their actions. Healthy families create a sense of belonging through positive cohesive bonds while respecting individual differences.

Children of alcoholics, however, attain their identity through blurred parental vision and poisoned parental verbiage. Mistakes are forbidden. Alcohol dilutes self-concept and shrivels self-esteem. In such households, children don't know where they stand. Monday's praised behavior is damned on Tuesday. Uncertain of what will happen next, many of these children become tiny, stiff soldiers always on guard, alert, anticipating problems for self-preservation. They are brave sentries fighting to control an uncontrollable situation. The alcoholic family's cohesion is criticism, violence, inconsistency, denial, and overwhelming stress. Survival replaces growth.

Accomplishments

In healthy families, parents continually acknowledge their children's accomplishments. Expectations are realistic, and encouragement is routine. Within this framework, parents establish firm boundaries and extend guidelines for their children.

Within the alcoholic family structure, however, the accomplishments of children receive acknowledgment depending on the mood of the alcoholic; therefore, criticism is frequent. Potential for physical, sexual, or verbal abuse bloats within household liquor bottles. Expectations are altered by levels of blood alcohol. Encouragement turns abusive with the arrival of the cocktail hour. Alcoholic families struggle to maintain order in a system in which inconsistency is the primary constant.

Denial

Denial is pervasive. The family that ignores an alcoholic member's behavior permits denial to produce make-believe. The "family secret" is protected by masks and careful dialogue. On stage, the children pretend to be normal. Often they are the honor-roll son or blue-ribbon daughter: boys and girls trying to be what they think they "should be" to protect themselves and the family's image. Lucy, the middle-aged daughter of an alcoholic father, described her denial pattern this way: "All my life I peeked out from behind cardboard bodies. I made the bodies myself, painting on faces and clothes for different occasions. I didn't know what I was doing, I only knew I was scared. With my teachers I was one 'Lucy,' with the minister another. When I got married, another 'Lucy' was taken out. All of a sudden I was fifty years old and had all these bodies. There were too many others and too little me."

Teachers have difficulty spotting one of these youngsters. "How could anything be out of order at Brenda's home?" a teacher might ask. "She's such a good student and so well behaved." But Brenda is like the duck in the pond. She glides across the water, but must frantically paddle underneath it to do so.

Amidst frenzy and inconsistency, children of alcoholics seldom learn how to predict the sane outcome of an action. A "by-the-seat-of-the-pants" problem-solving technique (stimulus/response quickly executed) is devised without thought of its consequences. The resulting turmoil sparks further confusion, until you eventually become an intensity junkie who is hooked on excitement. Days for these children are states of flux parading as normal. Pandemonium becomes the familiar.

Fear

Fear, too, becomes the familiar, a sense of doom that envelops the child like darkness. The unpredictability of parental expectations and reactions creates a palpable fear of the unknown. What will set Dad off today? Will Mom be drunk when I get home from school? What will I get blamed for tonight? "I've been afraid as long as I can remember," said Sharrie, the daughter of an alcoholic mother. "As a child I felt everything was my fault, and I remember being afraid that someone would find out." And like many children of alcoholics, Sharrie, as an adult, knows an anxiety that disguises reality. The anxiety is sometimes undefinable, most times unexplainable, and it forces Sherrie to walk through her days terrified of a "something" she cannot even name.

Like fear of the unknown, fear of another's anger is also intense for children in an environment controlled by alcohol. For anger in such a home is irrational. It is shouting and screaming and someone being blamed. It is sometimes hitting. Exposure to maniacal outbursts teaches children they should do anything to avoid confrontation. Simon, the son of alcoholic parents, speaks of what happens in his life now having learned that message as a boy: "When I'm around someone who's angry, even though I'm thirty-four, my whole body tenses. I'm terrified and I run away. It's like I'm eight years old again hearing my parents scream at each other. I have to get away as fast as I can, just as I used to."

Guilt

Experiencing anger and criticism, children growing up with an alcoholic parent will often assume layers of guilt. Many decide they are at fault for their drinking parent's behavior, or that they should be able to stop it. "If only I were smarter (or less shy, or a better athlete), then Daddy wouldn't get mad and drink so much." And as adults, many of these children continue to feel guilty a major portion of the time—forever assuming blame, forever apologizing.

Some adult children carry guilt for childhood thoughts or actions. Tony said, "I remember being about fourteen and thinking, 'I wish my father were dead; then all my problems would go away.' What kind of a kid wishes that?" Or Linda: "One night my mom was drunk and really going after me. I went to bed and pretended to go to sleep, but she came into my room, leaned over me, and continued to holler. Well, I hauled off and punched her in the face." For years Linda didn't allow herself to believe anything was unusual with her mother. Instead, she told herself that she was at fault. On some level, Linda chose to feel guilty instead of feeling angry. Did guilt feel safer?

In the chaotic alcoholic environment, little is safe and controllable. Mom and Dad can't be trusted, daily life is unpredictable, painful feelings are repressed, and emotions are parceled out with suspicion and adapted to the situation. As the daughter of an alcoholic father said: "Growing up as I did, I had to replace skin with armor." Children with alcoholic parents expend exorbitant energy to just be.

THE BURDENS OF THE PAST

Sadly, the pattern creeps into adult life. Shadows from the alcoholic home often follow these children into adulthood as fear, guilt, anger, emptiness, loneliness, helplessness, hopelessness, depression, sadness, worthlessness, suspiciousness, and a sense of being different from others. Unhealed adult children of alcoholics carry grotesque burdens.

Below you will see a chart that can help you establish the amount of time you are in pain over these burdens. Number one on the graph represents none of the time. Number ten represents all of the time. Analyze each state and mark the point that corresponds to the amount of time you experience pain concerning the state.

Feeling	None of the time								All of the time
	1	2	3	4	5	6	7	8	9	10
guilt									
fear									
anger									
emptiness									
loneliness									
helplessness									
hopelessness									
depression									
sadness									
worthlessness									
wariness									
sense of being different									

After you have finished, draw a line connecting the numbers together. Then shade the area to the left of the line. The amount of shading you see gives you a general idea of the amount of time you're experiencing pain within these states. To help you, here is the way Anne, the daughter of an alcoholic father, worked the exercise. However, before she did she commented: "It was months after joining an Adult Children of Alcoholics Al-Anon group before I could identify these states. We adult children have suppressed our feelings with things like alcohol, food, and casual sex for so many years it's difficult to recognize real feelings."

If you are unable to distinguish these states, put the exercise aside for a while. If you would like to do the work, here is Anne's graph to help you:

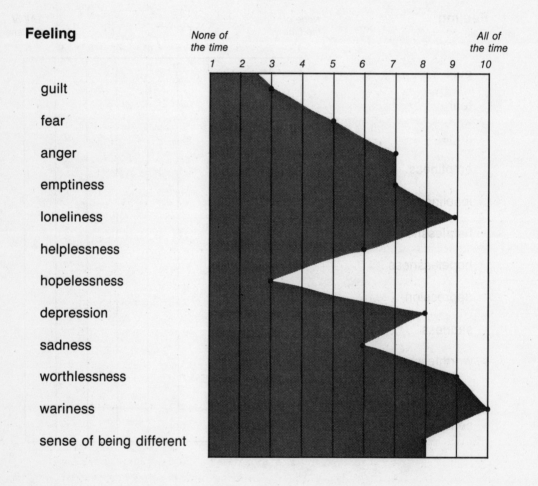

Feeling

None of the time   *All of the time*

1   2   3   4   5   6   7   8   9   10

guilt

fear

anger

emptiness

loneliness

helplessness

hopelessness

depression

sadness

worthlessness

wariness

sense of being different

ACKNOWLEDGING THE PAST

To unburden yourself, you must first acknowledge the wounds from your past. An identified bruise can be soothed and salved. Without blaming anyone, you can pinpoint areas that need healing by recalling childhood memories. Exercises in the next chapter aid the process by helping you bring these memories to the surface.

Bill, an adult child of an alcoholic, shared how he acknowledged a childhood memory and advanced his recovery.

> All my life, whenever I'd close my eyes, the people around me were ten feet tall and I wasn't; my co-workers, my wife, even my children. Out of fear and defeat I hid in a shell for over thirty years.
>
> About four months after I joined an adult children's Al-Anon meeting, an old memory came back. In it I was five years old. I was sitting at the dining room table surrounded by big parents, big sisters, and a big grandpa. Everyone looked ten feet tall. The message I got was that little people should be quiet or else big people would make fun of them.
>
> In the beginning I tried to push the memory away, but it kept coming back and it hurt. I stopped going to the Al-Anon meeting and returned to my shell tactic. But that didn't work either. So I looked at the memory again and decided to go past it and be new. For the first time, holding that memory, the ten-feet-tall people around me made sense. With my new understanding they didn't scare me any more. Now, when I close my eyes, one or two people are nine feet tall but most have come down all the way. It wasn't courage. It was a "want" to be who I could be. I walked out of my shell to be something more. But first I had to walk away from that dining room table.

———————————

Like Bill, many adult children remain trapped in childhood perceptions that contribute to present dysfunction and distress.

When they begin to look back, many adult children notice that they have few childhood memories. If that is your experience, accept it without concern. You may work the exercises with the material you do remember, or you might choose to postpone certain exercises. You can return to the room of your authentic self for assistance. There's no right way, just your way. Every moment of your life you possess what you need at the time. When you need more memories, they will be there.

Some adult children gather early photo albums to help unearth memories. Others have written to aunts, uncles, or siblings asking questions to get an added sense of the family personality. But understand these are ancillary suggestions. To do the exercises you only have to have the desire to get well. You too can walk beyond the past to become, like Bill, something "more."

————————————

Chapter 3

Childhood Environment

I have the power to choose my own destiny,
aware of my goodness and the goodness of life.

In a moment you will return to your childhood setting. This chapter will help you explore the past as you reexperience people, places, and traditions. You will be asked to recall the home of your childhood. If you lived in a number of homes, choose one to work with.

When you work, pace yourself. Don't rush. Chapter 3 might be the place to consider using a timer. Recovery means to come home to yourself in peace, not out of breath.

EXERCISE #4

The Protected Chair

Please take your workbook and a pencil to a comfortable chair. Relax. Close your eyes and say to yourself, *I breathe in eternal peace.* As you did in chapter 1, hold the breath for a moment, then exhale, saying, *I breathe out eternal peace.* Repeat the procedure substituting the words "eternal harmony" and "eternal love."

Concentrate on the breath. If you wish, you may use the relaxation exercise from the first chapter. Starting with your toes, say to yourself, *My toes are going to relax, they are relaxing, they are relaxed.* Relax each part of your body, ending with your scalp.

When you are ready, imagine that your chair is a safe chair that is sealed in a protective bubble. You feel secure in the chair; nothing can harm you. Breathe the security. You are relaxed and at peace.

Notice the breath, the even rhythm in and out. Then allow your special chair to propel you into space. You float peacefully. You travel until you reach the neighborhood of your youth. Trees on your childhood street come into view. You recognize friends and neighborhood pets. Relax and feel the breath entering and exiting the nostrils.

You see the house you grew up in, its surrounding lawn and gardens. Float in your protected chair through the roof of the house and come to rest in the living room. When you feel comfortable, let your internal eyes wander the room, scanning familiar objects and pieces of furniture. Breathe peacefully.

Begin the exercises when you feel you are ready. You may do as many or as few of the exercises as you wish. When you want to stop working and return to your adult environment, merely ask your chair to take you home. It will do so at once.

Part 1—Places

To help you awaken memories, this first section invites you to revisit rooms in your childhood home and draw pictures or write statements about those rooms. If you would like to do that, stay in your protected chair while the workbook guides you from room to room. Some adult children find benefit in writing down incidents that took place in the rooms. Spaces are provided if you choose to do that.

Example
To demonstrate, I have drawn a picture of the living room in the house where I was raised.

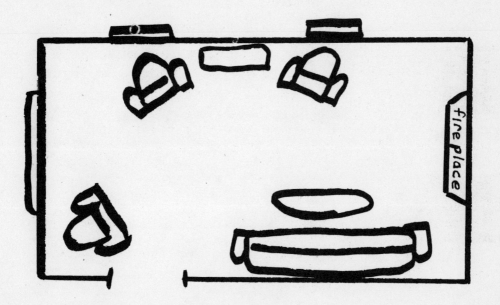

Incidents that occurred in the room:

Being surprised to find a book of poems in my Christmas stocking when I was five years old and certain that I deserved coal.

Spilling a bottle of blue ink on the living room carpeting.

If you want to unearth memories by revisiting your childhood rooms, please start with the living room. When you have finished with that, allow your protected chair to move you to other rooms in the house.

CHILDHOOD LIVING ROOM

Incidents

CHILDHOOD DINING ROOM

Incidents

CHILDHOOD KITCHEN

Incidents

You may continue to journey through the house, or, if you prefer, you may ask the protected chair to return you to your adult environment. It will do so immediately. Make the exercise fit your needs.

PARENTS' BEDROOM

Incidents

MY BEDROOM

Incidents

OTHER IMPORTANT ROOMS

Incidents

Part 2—People

Be proud of yourself for the work you completed. Going into the past demands courage; getting better takes energy and can be painful. So often, what I need to do, I want to avoid. But what I repress has the power to control me. As Eileen, an adult child, said, "I'm only as sick as my darkest secret."

When you are ready to continue your unburying process, you may begin the next section, which deals with family members in your childhood. It encourages memories by asking you to draw pictures of, or jot down ideas about, these people. If you have difficulty visualizing, and many people do, adapt these exercises to your best memory modes: auditory, emotional, kinesthetic, or tactile. Use what's right for you. If it helps, illustrate family members in the clothes you remember them wearing; write down each person's likes and dislikes; record their habits and hobbies.

You will notice that the segments dealing with your parents ask for some extra information. This is to further assist your memory, but you may complete as many or as few of the statements as you feel comfortable doing.

Example
To help you begin, I have drawn a picture of my father. I remembered him wearing cutoff jeans and sneakers without socks.

Likes: *Reading, yard work, children, and ice-cream sundaes*
Dislikes: *Arguing, gum chewing, and laziness*
Habits: *Getting up early in the morning, daily exercise*
Hobbies: *Stamp collecting and tennis*

A PICTURE OF MY FATHER

Likes:

Dislikes:

Habits:

Hobbies:

1. When my dad was happy about something I did, he rewarded me in these ways:

2. When my dad was angry over something I did, he punished me in these ways:

3. Things my father taught me to do:

4. My dad felt these values were the most important in life:

5. My dad felt these values were unimportant in life:

6. If I were to describe my father in one word, the word would be:

7. To my knowledge, my father's childhood was like this:

A PICTURE OF MY MOTHER

Likes:

Dislikes:

Habits:

Hobbies:

1. When my mother was happy about something I did, she rewarded me in these ways:

2. When my mom was angry over something I did, she punished me in these ways:

3. Things my mother taught me to do:

4. My mother felt these values were the most important in life:

5. My mom felt these values were unimportant in life:

6. If I were to describe my mother in one word, the word would be:

7. To my knowledge, my mother's childhood was like this:

PICTURES OF MY SISTERS

Likes:

Dislikes:

Habits:

Hobbies:

PICTURES OF MY BROTHERS

Likes:

Dislikes:

Habits:

Hobbies:

PICTURES OF OTHER PEOPLE WHO LIVED IN THE HOUSE WITH ME

Likes:

Dislikes:

Habits:

Hobbies:

Part 3—Family Traditions

The third section of this chapter invites memories by instructing you to recall family traditions. But again, don't rush. If you feel tired after working the previous sections, close the workbook and direct the protected chair to return you to your adult environment. Take time with your healing process.

1. My family celebrated these holidays:

2. What I wanted to happen during holiday celebrations was:

3. What usually happened during holidays was:

4. My most vivid memory of a holiday is:

5. I remember that holiday because:

6. My family celebrated birthdays this way:

7. I remember my birthdays the years I turned:

8. I remember those birthdays because:

Aware of the past, you may now return to the present. Ask your protected chair to float you through the roof of your childhood house. After you leave the house, travel above the neighborhood and across the sky. The protected chair gently returns you to your present environment.

———————

Having revisited the house you were raised in, recalled the people you grew up with, and recollected the traditions you celebrated as a child, you have probably awakened a number of memories. You may now investigate the childhood emotions and defense mechanisms those memories contain, and then restructure the old behavior patterns. Restructuring promotes recovery, and later chapters will assist you in this process.

Take time to be proud of yourself before you proceed. The honesty you brought to the exercises demonstrates courage and commitment. Feeling drained or tired is normal. If that's what you feel, walk quietly through the remainder of your day.

Perhaps you might like to reward yourself for having worked so hard. Take the dog for a walk, shop for a sweater, relax in a tub of hot water, or listen to your favorite music. Treating yourself is a restorative habit you've probably neglected. But before you scoot to the shopping mall or walk the dog, find a mirror and stare at yourself in the glass. Tell yourself how proud you are of you, how proud you are of the healthy work you are doing. Know you are special and say so out loud.

———————

Chapter 4

Beliefs and Adjustments

----

*I am a worthwhile person who lives life with patience
and understanding towards others and myself.*

One morning my family awoke to one of those spring blizzards that reminds us that we live in the Midwest. My children brought boots up from the basement and delighted in the free day from school. My husband unburied the snow shovel. As the storm continued, I did a little reading, then called some friends and asked them to share a snowy evening and a pot of homemade soup. To me, heavy snowfalls invite "coziness."

As I filled the soup kettle with water, I reached for a fortune cookie from the box my daughter had left on the counter. Cracking open the brittle cookie, I slipped the fortune from its shell—and stopped. Fortunes in the past had promised rich admirers or a future in the movies, material more suited to my daughter. The slip of paper I held that day read, "There is nothing in life except what we put there."

The soup bubbled, and I smiled. Some writer for a Chinese cookie company had encapsuled the thesis of my book. Indeed, there is nothing in the lives of adult children of alcoholics that adult children, themselves, didn't put there.

But what about the feelings of worthlessness? The cruelty? When you were young, you observed what was going on in your family, and, with the information you had at the time, you *believed* that everything was your fault. You *believed* that a parent was cruel or that no one could be trusted, and you told yourself that those beliefs were real. Granted, if there was alcoholism in your family, there was abnormal behavior. But you were the one who interpreted what was going on in your family, and your interpretations established the degree of abnormality.

Laura, an adult child, related this experience: "One night when I came home from a date, my mother was standing at the front door with her arms folded tightly across her chest. She had been drinking and was wild and furious. Eventually I learned that she'd been reading a bunch of letters I'd just written but hadn't mailed. She twisted everything around and accused me of terrible things. That was the night I determined I couldn't trust her or anyone else. I now believe it was the alcohol I couldn't trust, not my mother —but that didn't help back then."

To heal, you are asked to recall your early beliefs and claim responsibility for them. To do so does not negate your pain. But to get well you are asked to put the pain in perspective and to use your adult wisdom to resculpture your past beliefs.

Chapter 3 allowed you to explore your childhood and return to the present with memories of your early life. Chapter 4 asks you to spread those memories in front of you, to review them, and to recall your resulting beliefs.

Memories

Take a moment and write down some of the memories you uncovered in the previous chapter:

EARLY BELIEFS

Now look at your early beliefs surrounding those memories. Four common beliefs other adult children of alcoholics have discovered are these: I can't do anything right, I can't think straight, I can't trust anyone but myself, and I can't experience or express feelings.

I Can't Do Anything Right

This painful belief is often the result of the negative feedback children of alcoholics receive in the home. Again and again Johnny tries to "do" something to make Dad happy—but fails. Again and again Jean is criticized and told, through words or rolled eyes, that she doesn't measure up. Where there is alcohol abuse, there are judgment and blame.

Steven spoke of his "I-can't-do-anything-right" belief: "I remember being little, maybe four or five. My father let me help him and I was so proud. He was painting the kitchen, and he let me paint the door. Oh, I painted and painted. He was gone for a long time; I must have put three coats of paint on that door. It was a mess, but I wanted to please him so much. When he came back he was furious and yelled: 'You can't do anything right.' His words pierced me. Now I don't finish things. I'll get something almost done, then go on to something else. I have a wooden model of the ship, the *Constitution*, which is finished, except for a few deadeyes. It's been that way for fifteen years. I dust it, but I can't finish it. If I don't finish things, people can't yell at me."

Helen spoke of her "I-can't-do-anything-right" belief: "When I was a child, I had three or four imaginary friends. But my imaginary friends weren't like other people's. Mine used to beat me up. I never questioned what they did, because I believed that they knew that I was a goof-off, a loser."

After a few years of this conditioning, a child grows timid and cautious, refusing to take risks—afraid to go forward. Everything seems to be his fault, so guilt is commonplace. In the vacuum at the center of the "I-can't-do-anything-right" belief, self-esteem turns to dust and human potential lies fallow.

EXERCISE #5

In the space below, draw a picture or write a paragraph illustrating a childhood memory that shows an "I-can't-do-anything-right" belief.

I Can't Think Straight

Denial often encourages the "I-can't-think-straight" belief, because when a child experiences A but is told he experiences B, the mixed message confuses him and teaches him to distrust his own thought process. Distortion occurs when someone creates excuses for a parent's behavior—"Don't disturb your father this morning; he was up late last night,"—or when justifications are produced—"Daddy works so hard for us. You kids can understand why he needs to let loose once in a while, can't you?"

Ignoring the behavior also distorts clear thinking. "When I was a kid," Pauline said, "nobody said 'boo' about Mom's drinking. Dad, my two brothers, and I pretended everything was okay. Not one of us mentioned what was going on. I guess we thought that maybe the problem would go away if we acted as if things were normal. We did that the whole time I was at home."

If the behaviors are acknowledged in the alcoholic home, then the problems will be "real" and demand resolution. Instead, families of alcoholics frequently choose to ignore reality out of a need for self-preservation. To acknowledge reality is scary. Might not a family be overwhelmed and possibly destroyed? Also, to think straight and acknowledge the problem smacks of betrayal, and betrayal breeds guilt. To pretend seems safer than to protest.

In the alcoholic system, perceived self-protection invites an "I-can't-think-straight" belief.

EXERCISE #6

In the space below, draw a picture or write a paragraph illustrating a childhood memory that shows an "I-can't-think-straight" belief.

I Can't Trust Anyone But Myself

Children develop trust as the adults in their lives gradually satisfy their basic physical and emotional needs. But children who experience erratic parental behavior, endure alcohol-induced abuse, and tolerate inconsistent expectations eventually learn to distrust. Those children are guarded and apprehensive, and everyone is suspect.

Many adult children grew up afraid to bring friends into the home. Some experienced the terror of riding in a car with an intoxicated parent at the wheel. The possibility of a fire in the home was often present, as was the potential for physical, sexual, or verbal abuse. Fear pervaded and controlled daily life.

"I went to summer camp for a week when I was about nine years old," Ruth said. "When I got home at the end of the week, no one was there for me; my mom and dad were off at the bar. How awful that was. I also remember a time when I was six. I woke up one morning and wondered why our living room couch was outside on the lawn. I later found out that my dad had fallen asleep drunk with a cigarette in his hand. There was so little to trust in our family."

Trust emerges when surroundings are honest and safe, two conditions often absent in an alcohol-controlled environment.

EXERCISE #7

In the space below, draw a picture or write a paragraph illustrating a memory from your childhood that shows an "I-can't-trust-anyone-but-myself" belief.

I Can't Experience or Express Feelings

"My brother died of leukemia when he was nine years old, and I was ten. No one ever talked about it, it was like it never happened. My father would sit in the kitchen at night and drink and cry about my brother. I would feel so sorry for Dad. I wanted to help him, but we were never allowed to talk about feelings in our family," Cathy said.

And Nathan, an adult child, recalled: "When I was in grade school, I had a dog named Buddy. Buddy followed me everywhere. One night my father let the dog outside to run loose, something I never did because we lived on a highway, and Buddy was hit by a car. I was angry and upset, but when I told my father, he looked disgusted and yelled, 'If you really want to cry, I'll give you something to cry about.' That's about the time I began to believe that what I felt wasn't important. He was so big and talked so tough."

Children who grow up in alcoholic homes learn to repress their feelings. They learn this lesson from parents who refuse to deal with their own emotions, and from the criticism and ridicule they often receive when they try to express their own. Once again, an alcoholic environment encourages fantasy and denies reality.

"Often now," Tara said, "I think of how beautiful my mother was when she was younger. I wonder about all the fulfillment she has cheated herself out of because of alcohol. I really wonder what her life could have been like. She's so smart. I can't help but believe her entire life would have been totally different. I hate to say it was a waste, but it comes to mind first. I feel sad about that; but at least I am allowing myself to feel now, something I never did as a child."

EXERCISE #8

In the space below, draw a picture or write a paragraph illustrating a
memory from your childhood that shows an "I-can't-experience-
or-express-feelings" belief.

BEHAVIORAL ADJUSTMENTS

In an alcoholic environment, children's beliefs, four of which were just elaborated, generate heavy *shoulds* and *should nots.* For example, you may have believed that you should be silent and strong, should always appear happy, and shouldn't discuss the family outside the home. Following those *shoulds* and *should nots* and wanting what every child wants (to be loved), you made *adjustments* regarding what you thought would make you lovable. *And when I am lovable,* you believed, *I will have stability, security, and self-worth.*

In a moment you will be asked to recall and record some of the childhood behavioral adjustments you made in order to be accepted and loved. Here are some adjustments other adult children have discovered: I won't be me; I will pretend I'm happy; I will be quiet about what goes on at my house.

To assist you in remembering, Pietra, forty-nine, recalls her nightmarish existence from infancy to age twelve. Although her drunken uncle was forcibly removed from her home when she was twelve, she still struggles with her inner admonitions concerning self-esteem, clear thinking, trusting, and feeling. When she was a child, her entire extended family conspired to protect the alcoholic member by not dealing with the reality of his illness. Pietra realized very young that it was disloyal to the *whole* family to criticize the uncle's behavior.

"Even though my uncle was murderously violent, wielding guns, knives, and axes," Pietra said, "there was a conspiracy in our home that was extremely potent. An aunt who had married into our family dared to discuss 'family business' (her brother-in-law's alcoholism) with a neighbor. The whole family turned on her. I never understood why she was so vehemently and universally hated until I realized she had committed the ultimate taboo —acknowledging the problem and sharing it. I couldn't put this all into words back then, but I was smart enough to figure out that you don't mention such things if you want to be loved by the family!"

EXERCISE #9

Part 1

Recall the early ways you tried to be lovable.

To be lovable I felt I had to be
      Pietra: *Part of the conspiracy of silence.*

    You:

To be lovable I felt I could not be
      Pietra: *Myself.*

    You:

The Hurt

Part 2

Please draw a picture or write a paragraph illustrating what you did to be loved at ages six, twelve, and seventeen. Pietra again offers her examples.

Age six

Pietra:

adhesive tape

You:

Age twelve

Pietra: *Thank God, at twelve, I was finally free of my alcoholic uncle, but I was still afraid to bring friends home. It was as if his ghost still haunted my environment. Even though he moved only a few miles away, I never saw him or talked about him ever again, because to do either would have meant being disloyal to the family. At age twelve I decided to ignore what had happened in order to be loved by my family.*

You:

Age seventeen

> **Pietra:** *At seventeen I was still ashamed, still afraid to talk about "it." I had become painfully "shy" outside the family setting. At age seventeen I decided to become shy to be loved.*

You:

NEW BELIEFS

Inhale a healing breath and relax for a moment. If you're feeling uneasy, honor the discomfort, but know it is temporary. Early stages of healing can feel unpleasant. Trust who you are and what you're experiencing.

When you want to continue, refer back to the memories you recorded on page 57 of this chapter. Review them from the viewpoint of an adult who understands that alcoholism is a disease.

Also look at them as an adult who is learning that "I can't" now means "I won't." The difference is vital. What you believed you couldn't do in childhood mutates into what you won't do as an adult. For example, you may have believed you couldn't express anger when you were ten and had been sent to your room for losing your temper; but as an adult, you can choose to deal or not to deal with angry feelings. "I won't" means "I choose not to." You can only reach "I will" by stepping from "I won't." There's never a direct progression from "I can't" to "I will." Applying that knowledge and your knowledge of alcoholism as a disease, write new beliefs and new understandings about being lovable.

New beliefs might include a sentence like this: *I can think and acknowledge what I feel without being disloyal to anyone.* Or this: *Reality in the alcoholic home is illness, not evil.*

New understandings about being lovable could include a statement like this: *I can talk about my feelings and still be lovable.* Or this: *I can be who I am and be lovable.*

Feeling awkward as you rewrite early beliefs and understandings about being lovable is common, but focus on completing the exercise. Restructuring will release you from the bondage of fear. Repeating the chapter's affirmation might be helpful: *I am a worthwhile person who lives life with patience and understanding towards others and myself.* You might consider saying aloud: "I can stand what I'm feeling, feelings are transitory. I, not my emotions, am in charge of my thoughts and actions."

Be patient with yourself. Positive energy will replace those uncomfortable feelings, and hope will replace the despair.

EXERCISE #10

New beliefs

New understandings about being lovable

"There is nothing in life except what we put there."

Chapter 5

Self-Protection Roles

I claim my birthright to happiness and harmony.

"If this workbook promotes healing, why don't I feel better?"

Sound familiar? If it does, you're not alone. Most people feel worse when they start to get better. The experience is unfamiliar, and you feel exposed, vulnerable, scared, angry, and sad. Letting go of the past and what might have been is painful. But you can't buy recovery; you have to grow it. And if you've ever gardened, you know that preparing the soil can be a tiring, agonizing job. Healing, like gardening, can cause initial discomfort.

Healing also takes time. You didn't develop the behaviors that complicate your life in a month or a year. Don't expect to heal them and feel better in a few chapters. Getting well means committing yourself to the recovery process (including its pain) without deadlines. Discomfort is important because it signals growth. If you've ever had surgery, recalling the healing procedure might be useful. A few years ago I had major abdominal surgery. I checked into the hospital anxious to have a lot of pain relieved, but in order to rid myself of the symptoms of the problem, I had to live through the price of surgery: incisional pain, disrupted activities, weeks in bed. In the process of getting better, I had to put up with the discomfort of healing.

This workbook does not have to be your only recovery tool. Healing techniques are varied and plentiful, so consider using others to supplement it. You only need awareness to find them. Each day, for instance, offers potential healing tools: the song of a bird, the wind, the freshness of spring. You hear the cardinal and, with awareness, can know that life is good. You may want to experiment with the healing potential of music, art, or spirituality. Support groups, counseling, or Al-Anon meetings offer powerful healing—safe places where you can share your innermost feelings.

A therapeutic friend can facilitate your healing. You discover if a friend is "therapeutic" by identifying your feelings after sharing a particular problem with the person. Do you wind up feeling betrayed, discounted, or helpless? If you do, this isn't someone to confide in. A therapeutic friend is a person who listens without judgment or conditions, someone who makes you feel comfortable, not vulnerable. Then, having opened yourself to further healing tools and a realistic recovery program, continue with the workbook.

FAMILY ROLES

When you were little, you needed to feel loved and protected by the significant people in your life. To fill those needs you discovered "ways of being" (roles) that assured you of love and protection. If you were lucky, you chose a role that was positive. But positive or negative, your role was a way to take care of the emotional needs you had at the time. On occasion, your role took the focus off your alcoholic parent and placed it on yourself. It established balance for you amidst confusion and, on occasion, offered the outside world a positive statement reflecting a family image you felt called upon to protect. Again, you were a kid doing your best to survive.

In *The Family Trap: No One Escapes from a Chemically Dependent Family*, Sharon Wegscheider describes the four roles that children in alcoholic families assume for self-protection.[1] When you look at the categories, understand that although you refined one of them, you probably slipped in and out of all four at various times in your life.

As an adult, you need to recognize when you began to play the role (its origin) and how you felt about it (its ultimate expense). One way to detect the expense of a role is to isolate the feelings it produced: happiness, excitement, anger, fear, sadness. Identifying where in my body I have the feeling helps me, and may help you, isolate the feeling and understand its expense. Anger produces tension in my shoulders, neck, or head. I feel sadness in my throat. Fear is a game of marbles in my stomach. Excitement is a butterfly bursting from my abdomen into my rib cage. Happiness is a warmth on my skin. When I look at my role and remember the marble game in my stomach that accompanied it, I know the role's expense was living in fear. The exercises that follow invite you to remember what your role cost you. Body identification might be helpful for you.

The Family Hero

To begin, study the role that Sharon Wegscheider describes as the Family Hero. The Family Hero is the family "star." Heroes are often the oldest or only children. Exhibiting exemplary behavior, they honor their families through achievements as students or leaders, and they earn praise by assuming adult tasks, like preparing meals or taking care of siblings. Heroes are capable and accomplished, and they make the family shine. Children in this role are organized and efficient; they appear responsible and mature.

Sounds wonderful. What's wrong with being a "star"? Stars add stability to a household and achieve personal success. Aren't these desirable benefits? But consider the trade-offs, the expenses. There are loneliness and fear, and there's expressed or unexpressed anger. As the Family Hero, you always had to "do." If you assumed this role, you were chronically exhausted from "doing."

EXERCISE #11

If Family Hero was your role, write down your memories as Hero in the spaces that follow. Brenda, a physician, offers some examples.
How I acted as the Family Hero

> **Brenda:** *Superior scholastic achievement; as a teenager, I relished opportunities to appear mature by caring for younger brothers and sisters and doing household chores.*

> **You:**

Expense of being the Family Hero (how I ended up feeling)

   Brenda: *Afraid of both success and failure; sad (alone at the top).*

   You:

Other consequences of being the Family Hero

   Brenda: *Distancing myself from others because of my need to be the best; if I had any little failure, I felt (and feel) worthless.*

   You:

The Family Scapegoat

Family Scapegoats are troublemakers. Often second children, youngsters in this role are defiant and "prickly" to be near. They may break the law, get pregnant (or get someone pregnant), associate with wild friends, and begin to use drugs and alcohol early. Scapegoats seek self-importance outside the family.

If you took on this role, you were probably difficult to understand and impossible to discipline. "I'll show you," your actions said. "I'll do things my way." Most likely you seldom listened to others and often blocked their attempts at closeness.

As a troublemaker, you diverted the emphasis from the alcoholic to yourself. You cried for attention, and negative attention fulfilled an emotional need. Many outsiders blamed your deviant behavior for all your family's problems.

EXERCISE #12

Was your role the Family Scapegoat? If so, record your memories in the spaces that follow.

How I acted as the Family Scapegoat

Expense of being the Scapegoat (how I ended up feeling)

Other consequences of being the Family Scapegoat

The Lost Child

Wegscheider's third category is the Lost Child. Lost Children isolate themselves for self-protection. Often living in fantasy, they are quiet, dreamy, and ethereal. Some come to believe their fantasies, and lies become truth for these children. Attempting to deal with them in reality is like dancing with smoke.

Most Lost Children, wanting peace at any cost, become agreeable and appeasing, so they don't offer opinions and they never question anything. They are the "good little boys" or the "perfect little girls," never drawing attention to themselves, never causing concern. They are the adept adapters.

If you were a Lost Child, you probably blended into the walls like watercolor on paper. You never thought of causing trouble, preferring to withdraw into your room and yourself. Out of self-protection you sought safety in solitude. And what did you find?

EXERCISE #13

If the Lost Child was your role, record your memories in the spaces below.

How I acted as the Family Lost Child

Expense of being the Lost Child (how I ended up feeling)

Other consequences of being the Lost Child

The Family Mascot

The Family Mascot is Wegscheider's fourth identified role. Mascots make everyone laugh and feel jolly; they spring handstands or spin spontaneous anecdotes. On stage and overactive, they entertain while defusing the tension the alcoholic creates. When the focus is on frivolity, problems seem to disappear with whimsical wit. Humor rules and charisma represses.

If you were the Family Mascot, you were the family Medicine Man Show. You were scared and lonely, and yet the show had to go on, and on, and on.

EXERCISE #14

If the Family Mascot was your role, record your memories in the spaces that follow.

How I acted as the Family Mascot

Expense of being the Family Mascot (how I ended up feeling)

Other consequences of being the Family Mascot

FULFILLING YOUR NEEDS

When you were a child, you perfected a particular role or you aligned with two or three. But at one time or another, you probably tested all four. For instance, you may have been the Family Hero, but discovered some advantage to the Mascot's sense of humor and incorporated that trait into your own personality. Perhaps you were the Lost Child until your parents divorced, and then maybe the Scapegoat role fit your needs. The roles were open-ended and could be combined.

Within alcohol-controlled families, these roles do not line up in a particular pattern. Having four children in a family does not mandate four different roles. "It was weird," said adult child Julie. "I have two sisters and each of us was a Family Hero. Not one of us got into the supposedly negative roles."

You may have exchanged roles by choice or in response to change within the family. Roselyn, an adult child, spoke of the changes in her family and her choices: "There were eight kids in my family, but I was the one who was always in trouble. I guess you'd say I was the Scapegoat. Alice, my older sister, was the Family Hero. When Mom and Dad would get roaring drunk, Alice used to call the police and have them arrested. After Alice got married, I decided to take her place. One night when Mom and Dad were really bad, I tried to call the police, as Alice had done, but Dad grabbed the phone from my hand and pulled it out of the wall. It was like he wouldn't let me be the Hero; that was reserved for Alice. So, since I couldn't be the good guy, I settled into the Mascot role. At least that was safer than always getting into trouble as the Scapegoat."

No matter what your role was, you were a child coping with awkward surroundings. You devised ways to be safe amidst confusion. There was no "one" way. There was no "right" way. You did what you did to survive, and you survived. Now you are an adult, and you can choose what you will be with others.

EXERCISE #15

Take a moment to relax. When you are comfortable, write a poem or short paragraph about you and your self-protection role. Before you begin, consider how your role, or roles, filled your emotional needs. How did your choices make you feel lovable or attract the attention you desired? This is your story, your history, an important statement about who you are. You may want to draw pictures to help tell your story.

To help you, here is Cassie's poem.

A Lost Child
Loneliness is extreme.
Sitting on the curb of a street corner crying,
Waking at night crying,
Hiding in the shadows, or bedroom.
Tears, tears, and still tears.
Seems there was never anyone there to soften them.
And so now I want to buy a pink dress,
A light pink dress with dark flowers
And green fuzzy leaves.
I want to be pretty
Like I wanted to be pretty so my father
Would love me
So I could be his princess
Tears, tears, and still tears.

Your words

Chapter 6

Role Embellishments

I am at peace—and offer all creation
compassion and goodwill.

Once upon a time I decided to be a Hero. I wore my decision with grace, for I felt the role commanded respect and love. The robe of the Hero displayed my self-worth. Once upon a time, out of my awareness, I chose to *become* rather than to *be*.

My decision was probably similar to your decision. Also, my results. A chosen role satisfied our perceived childhood needs, but it stifled development of the genuine self. You and I became Heroes, Scapegoats, Lost Children, and Mascots out of the need for self-protection and unaware of long-term effects. In adult life, our heavy robes smother authenticity and mask pain.

EMBELLISHING OUR ROLES

But we not only wear robes, we embellish them. To validate our roles, you and I rationalized our care-giving, people-pleasing, long-suffering, and other behaviors. But these behaviors now seem affected. We've overdeveloped them, and they now hinder our ability to function as adults.

Isolating and examining your behaviors can assist your recovery process. You will be able to detect various embellishments: overachieving, care-giving, people-pleasing, being a perfectionist, long-suffering, antagoniz-ing, being a nobody. Concentrate on each when it is presented in the chapter, asking yourself questions such as these: Did being an overachiever (or care-giver, etc.) help me accomplish my role? Does being an overdevel-oped overachiever (or care-giver, etc.) complicate my present growth?

Being whole requires you to modify and sometimes discard out-of-proportion behaviors in your personality. Doing so allows you to begin making healthy choices. Imagine that your right arm represents "caring for others." Muscles in that arm bulge from years of development. You trained well, so your right arm is powerful. But the left arm, the arm that represents "caring for yourself," is weak. It hangs limp with underde-veloped muscle tissue. *Wholeness* means arms of equal strength. Wholeness is balance. Chapter 6 invites you to recognize and balance your actions.

To be whole also requires being aware of rebounds, opportunities we give ourselves for failure and self-punishment. When you allow a healthy behavior (e.g., achieving) to get out of balance (by pursuing the unattaina-ble), you set yourself up for a rebound (defeat). Rebounds are nasty, for they encourage self-hatred. "See, I knew it all along. I'm incapable. I'm unlovable." As you study your behaviors, be aware of how and when you manipulate them into destructive rebounds.

When you are ready, acknowledge the behaviors that apply to you, and dismiss those that do not. Acknowledging out-of-proportion behavior is critical. You must acknowledge so you can restructure in preparation for making healthy choices. If you need assistance, you may return to the room of your authentic self (chapter 1) for guidance. At all times trust who you are and what you know.

Overachieving

To further a chosen role, did you become an overachiever? Did you tell yourself something along these lines? If I make the honor roll, or become a basketball star, people will love me. Everyone loves a superstar. Right, Dad? Mom? Look at what I can do!

But did the affirmation you received feel like enough? Carol, an adult child of an alcoholic father, expressed her need this way: "All I ever wanted was to be loved. But I never feel I get enough love from anyone, and I exhaust myself trying to earn it. My pattern is to try again and again to become more and more—for love." If you became an overachiever, you too pushed and struggled and tried harder. See the scholarship. It proves I'm a winner. Now will you love me?

As adults, many overachievers become workaholics who see themselves as being only as valuable as the work they accomplish. But work, for workaholics, is never completed. They rush from task to task, driven, unable to rest, consumed by the need to tackle projects for elusive self-esteem.

Childhood overachievers err by believing that self-esteem comes from *doing*. When you carry that belief and continue that practice into maturity, you use yourself up like dust in a flame. You never satisfy the perceived standards, so you crumble after each disillusioned attempt. If I make over forty thousand dollars, I'll be lovable. If I become supermom, I'll be appreciated. If I write a book, I'll be worth something.

EXERCISE #16

If you suspect you became an overachiever to gain acceptance and love, list the areas where you had (and may still have) this tendency.

Care-Giving

To feel lovable, some children of alcoholics become care-givers. These young people feel worthwhile when they soothe another's physical or emotional pain. Care-giving develops when children tend their younger brothers and sisters or look after their parents. In Pam's words, "I remember being in high school and believing I had to take care of my father when my mother was drunk. I saw my role as protector and mediator. I remember Dad coming into my room at night to tell me how horrible things were. I felt I had to help him."

If you were a care-giver, you may have believed your self-esteem increased in proportion to your selflessness. While selfless motivated care for another deserves applause, this type of care-giving is not *selfless*. It is caring for another out of the need to look or feel good ourselves and, therefore, be loved and accepted.

In adulthood, many out-of-balance care-givers buzz around plumping pillows and applying Band-Aids under the guise of "charity." In unhealed care-givers, however, "plumping" and "applying" are more selfish than charitable.

Good works, of course, can help others even if the motive is misguided. Danger is present, though, when you do not recognize your subconscious intentions. Here's Pam again: "I learned to get people to like and approve of me by doing things for them. It was even better when I did things without being asked."

If you are an unhealed care-giver, you need to care for people in order to overcome a self-esteem deficiency. Here lies the danger. Out of your hunger for self-worth, do you establish relationships with weak or needy people? If you do, be careful because this practice encourages one of care-giving's rebounds: unhealed care-givers need the needy, and many adult children of alcoholics, being unhealed care-givers, submerge themselves in unhealthy relationships that are doomed from the beginning.

Unhealed care-givers also discount other people. They wear an "I-know-more-than-you-do" attitude, playing "yes but" and "you're incapable." Such individuals appear arrogant, and arrogance creates distance.

Another rebound is burnout. Overdeveloped care-givers exhaust themselves because their need for self-esteem requires complex involvement in the lives of others.

EXERCISE #17

If you suspect you became a care-giver to gain acceptance and love, list the areas where you had (and may still have) this tendency.

People-Pleasing

Craving love and wanting self-worth, children of alcoholics sometimes become people-pleasers who sacrifice selfhood for peace and shallow esteem. They can't allow anger in themselves or others, so they literally grind out tranquility. Pietra said: "Anger is a gun going off in the basement, an axe in a bedroom door. For me anger is life and death. I'm still controlled by my fear of anger. Where might it lead?"

Other young people-pleasers stand guard anticipating, and then satisfying, the needs of those around them—guessing then genuflecting. If I sense what you want (by reading your mind), if I nod and agree and serve you, will you love me? When you love me, I won't be abandoned. And when you keep me, then I'll know I'm worth something. People-pleasing takes tremendous energy.

Adult people-pleasers appear affected, and in a way they are. To placate and pacify others, overdeveloped people-pleasers must be artificial. Satisfying and winning approval of others requires suppressing and denying their own honest feelings. The resulting self-deprivation fires rage in their hearts, though it is a rage that is unconscious, unfelt, and unexpressed.

Consumed with anger beyond their awareness, some adult people-pleasers harden, becoming manipulative and mean. They repeat to themselves, *It's a rough world out there; I'd better protect myself by being tough.* Once again an early coping mechanism, overdeveloped, rebounds into a self-devouring monster.

Did you distort reality and discount your own needs out of a desperate desire for safety, harmony, and harmony's promised gift of self-worth?

EXERCISE #18

If you suspect you became a people-pleaser, list the areas where you had (and may still have) this tendency.

Perfectionism

Perfectionism is another behavior some children exhibit. To meet assumed parental demands, perfectionists try to attain excellence in all that they do. They feel they have to be perfect in order to be lovable, so they continue to say things like "See my perfect report card, Daddy. Do my perfect disposition/demeanor/dress/date/diction/denial please you? Will you love me now?"

Adult child Essie said: "I was never able to vocalize the need I felt to be perfect; or, that my need to be perfect was a need for my father's love. All I sensed was this undefined longing. It was a longing that drove me to the refrigerator night after night, a hunger that could never be fulfilled."

On being a young perfectionist with an alcoholic father, Tom recalled: "I had to be perfect as a child. I would lie or embellish to make others think I was perfect, especially when I got older. But perfection was impossible because my parents kept changing the criteria."

Many adult children practice perfectionism today, seeking unreachable, unattainable goals. "I will be the perfect mother." "I will sell more insurance than anyone else." Living perfectionism assures defeat because accomplishments do not satisfy: they could have been more important, more flashy, more like Susie's. Perfectionists compete and compare, and when they don't measure up to others, they beat themselves raw. "I always have this feeling," Claire said, "that I must be perfect in everything. I feel sad and guilty when I'm not. Then, feeling guilty, I usually punish myself. I take pills or overeat, anything that proves I'm a loser."

EXERCISE #19

If you suspect you became a perfectionist to attain love and acceptance, list the areas where you have (and may still have) this tendency.

Long-Suffering

To develop a role, did you become a long-sufferer, a person who feels worthwhile because of what, and how well, you endure?

Living with an alcoholic parent did require strength. Children in that environment experience substantial stress and are asked to tolerate intolerable behavior, so they devise mechanisms to relieve the tension and foster the self-esteem they desire. But when an adult seeks self-esteem through out-of-balance martyrdom, the potential for a painful rebound awaits. Joyce, an adult child, expressed her unhealthy behavior this way: "All my life I felt sorry for myself and used sympathy for attention. I loved it when others patted my head in compassion. I still love it. 'Poor Joyce' gets me a lot of recognition, but it feeds an ugly self-pity."

After long-sufferers grow up, most continue, unaware, to crave unpleasant situations, and some adult children unconsciously choose suffering as a means to get attention. Attention, for these people, means survival: neglect is death. Some, therefore, will not only crave unpleasant situations; they will create them. A mechanism that once helped a child cope successfully rebounds destructively in the adult. Adults who retain these inappropriate coping mechanisms find it difficult to achieve what they consciously want when their unconscious, conditioned needs take over. You may want to be happy, but when a deeper part of you needs to be unhappy, that part prevails and unhappiness is the result. Suffering, like many other behaviors, is unpleasant. But beware: on a deeper level you may perceive it as necessary for survival.

Quiet suffering creates security in an alcohol-laden environment, but to endure is to be passive. Long-suffering means sitting in problems, not having to solve them. Some unhealed martyrs continue to sit, since doing so seems safer than acting. Yet another rebound looms: when you don't solve your problems, you hide in ambivalence. You make no decisions, and no changes, so your ambivalence shrivels your potential.

Understand that suffering is optional.

EXERCISE #20

If you suspect you became a long-sufferer to gain acceptance and love, list the areas where you had (and may still have) this tendency.

Antagonizing

Another way to be noticed is to be an antagonist who picks and scratches for recognition. Cynical and sly as unhealed adults, antagonists began as innocent young people seeking love and attention. "Please notice I'm here," they say. "Look at me, not at the alcoholic."

Antagonists start fights and tell lies. They bully the neighbors and build boundaries that say "You are only allowed to come this close."

When antagonizing behavior is continued into adult life it creates many forms of dysfunction. Adult children practicing their antagonism are painfully lonely. Their anger is palpable, and relationships, when they are allowed, are disastrous. Alcoholism and drug abuse abound. For antagonists, self-esteem is self-loathing and self-destruction. Wanting to be loved, they make it impossible for anyone to approach them. And, unfortunately, they can end up incapable of loving.

EXERCISE #21

If you believe you became an antagonist to gain acceptance and love, list the areas where you had (and may still have) the tendency.

Being a Nobody

"When I was growing up," said Barbara, an adult child of alcoholic parents, "I felt like a nothing. My feelings didn't count, nor anything I did. In my family I was an observer looking in a window. I wasn't a worthy person. I felt no purpose in life and, for a while, no reason for living."

Some children in alcoholic homes, believing they're unwanted, become nobodies in order to be accepted. If I make no demands, if I'm out of the way, maybe you'll love me. If I have no needs, no feelings, maybe you'll care.

Young nobodies exist like still air—colorless and soundless. They believe they have been given a message: you are more important when you aren't here. "My translation was, 'If you commit suicide we'll be happier.' No one said it, I just felt it," said Carl, the son of an alcoholic father.

Adult children who remain nobodies as adults are lonely and angry. They don't know why they fail. They don't know what they need, and they cannot ask. Such loss of self invites immobilizing depression.

I wanted to be loved, so I got out of your way. But where did I put me?

EXERCISE #22

If you felt you had to be a nobody to gain love and acceptance, list the areas where you had (and may still have) this tendency.

RESTRUCTURING

Unless they are restructured, overdeveloped and overextended behaviors pepper life with anguish. Unbalanced, these behaviors feed negativity and keep you "stuck." Consequently, you may experience fear, guilt, self-judgment, distrust, sadness, unworthiness, rage, intimacy difficulties, addiction, inability to relax, and the need to control. To restructure is to acknowledge and moderate a behavior, because moderation heals wounds and encourages growth.

When I acknowledge a behavior, I claim it as part of my personality. For example, I first accept being an overachiever, then I put it in perspective. Overachieving, which began as a way to embellish my Hero role, helped me attain scholastic success for many years. It also helped me write this book. Those are healthy results. Trouble occurs when I feel I'm only as "good" as what I accomplish, or when I work so intensely that my family life, health, and peace of mind erode. Those are the rebounds. When I choose to moderate my out-of-proportion overachieving, I am aware that balanced behavior empowers my life. Finding new focus I write:

> *I like how overachieving taught me to set goals and to work hard to attain them. I will continue to be a hard worker, but I will no longer work as if driven. I accept that I am a valuable person for who I am, not for what I do. I will make a contract with myself to moderate my behavior by meditating twice a day and by setting up daily times for enjoyment with my husband and children.*

EXERCISE #23

To restructure an overdeveloped behavior, as I just did, write out your contract, or contracts, in the spaces that follow.

Overachieving

Care-Giving

People-Pleasing

Perfectionism

Long-Suffering

Antagonizing

Being a Nobody

Chapter 7

Sabotage and Self-Fulfilling Prophecies

---

*I possess everything I need, and I perceive the good
in everything I encounter.*

"In our adult lives the 'child of the past' is constantly trying to make us live
as we lived 'at home' in childhood. Due to this influence, we keep twisting
our present circumstances and relationships to resemble those we knew in
the past," writes Dr. Missildine in *Your Inner Child of the Past.*[1]

As damaging as their early lives were, adult children of alcoholics return
to the familiar and invite disaster. Unconsciously, they re-create the past.
Sixty percent become alcoholic. By ritualistically involving themselves in
unhealthy relationships, adult children of alcoholics satisfy a sick (but
familiar) need to be abandoned. "Because I feel unlovable," Ron said, "I
continually pick women who abuse me, proving what I already know."

THE NEEDS OF THE PAST

When you burn your hand on the stove, you learn a lesson: a hot stove
hurts. You won't burn your hand a second time—unless there is a "payoff."
The payoff, for some adult children, is that the pain from the stove feels
good because it is *familiar.*

The irony is that many adult children, having survived childhoods of chaos and having resolved never to live such agony again, not only *do* live agony, they create it. Adult children of alcoholics *burn their hands* over and over. They may say, "Not me. I'm too smart to end up like my father," but they do end up like Dad or Mom or Grandpa because there is a payoff in doing so. Adult children find what they need (familiar confusion and pain), not what they want (peace and happiness).

What is a need? The word, rather dull and limp-sounding, deceives. Explosive power coils between the *n* and the *d*: power with bite. You control what you want. What you need controls you. When your past is unhealed, it accompanies you in your daily reactions and urges. It influences simple decision making. Under the guise of necessity, the influence of the past is difficult to identify.

Everyone has basic needs for food, shelter, sleep. But because you are an adult child of an alcoholic, you may also have self-destructive needs. Due to early conditioning, you may need to feel worthless. You may need to punish yourself or to stagnate in self-pity. To fulfill a perceived need and feel comfortable may mean re-creating the familiar. And what are the familiar to an adult child? Abandonment. Fear. Inconsistency. Guilt. Isolation. Self-hatred. Needing to control.

Adult children choose these painful childhood playmates and well-worn playthings because they contain no surprises. You survived once; you will again. New behaviors are frightening and risky. "Hold it," you shout as you wave a burned hand. "Don't make me try something different. Fear and guilt are bad, but the unknown scares me more." And how can you return yourself to the familiar? Through alcoholism, eating disorders, violence, and intimacy problems.

For some people, living the known is comfortable compared to dealing with the unknown. Returning to childhood hearth and role models is fine for some individuals, but when adult children consciously or subconsciously choose early hearth and role models, in part they choose pain.

EXERCISE #24

Part 1

Relax. Inhale a cleansing breath and be present in the moment. Before you continue your healing journey, stop and experience your new awarenesses. Some of what you've learned is exciting; you finally make sense. Other material is painful and may make you uneasy. All your experiences are valuable because they are a part of you. Thank yourself for claiming your insights and for discarding what didn't apply to you. How wise you are.

Part 2

When you are ready, you are invited to do an exercise using a picture of yourself as a child. If a snapshot is available, good; if not, imagine how you looked as a young person. When you are ready to begin, concentrate on the image. Take your time. Experience the precious child in the photograph and know that that very child is still within you. The child has been with you since birth, aware of you even though you were unaware of it. Your adult self needn't feel afraid. The inner child loves you. It has helped you cope all these years. It now wants to help you by integrating itself and its wisdom into your mature personality. When you feel safe, talk to the child, introduce yourself, and say "thank you." Then listen and allow the child to introduce itself to you. When the child sees your respect and also feels safe, it will trust you and talk openly. But know that if you wish it to happen, it will happen.

If you aren't ready to communicate yet, the child will honor that. Sensing your discomfort, it may choose to talk to you in a dream, which *you* can choose to remember or forget.

To record the introductions, you may use the following space. If further space is needed, write in your journal or on a loose piece of paper. Other adult children have found using a tape recorder is helpful at this point.

Example
To help you, when I introduced myself to my inner child, the introduction went partially like this:
Patty: *"Inner child, I understand you've known and protected me all these years. But I feel awkward talking to you like this, it's such a new concept—yet I want to thank you for all that you've done. I now realize how important you have been in my life. I can't believe this is happening."*
Child: *"It sure is happening, and I'm glad it is. It's about time you knew I was here!"*

The Hurt

Your introduction

Part 3

After the two of you feel at ease, ask your inner child questions! Ask about early memories and behaviors, and use your journal to record your conversations. This ingenious part of yourself has always been aware of your needs, protections, and payoffs, and it can share valuable information. For example, when I asked my inner child why I smoked, it answered: "You smoke because you believe it is the only thing you can count on, Patty. Cigarettes to you are comfortable, faithful friends."

When you wish to continue with the workbook, gently say good-bye to your child but tell it that the two of you will talk again. Tell the child you are grateful for its openness.

RE-CREATING CHAOS

When adult children live unconscious of their self-destructive needs, those needs risk becoming self-fulfilling prophecies that re-create chaos. The following paragraphs detail some of the ways adult children stay stuck and invite the unwanted. Recognize your susceptibility to the past. Doing so, you can, if necessary, seek therapeutic help to deal with infecting behaviors, and you can alert yourself to the dangers inherent in other behaviors. Again, not every area listed will apply to you. With gentleness, claim what is yours and go on. If you wish, your inner child or the room of your authentic self can help you get under the behaviors to discover what you need to know to make recovery possible.

Alcoholism

Let's begin with alcoholism, a progressive disease that afflicts millions of people. It is the nation's number one problem in terms of socioeconomic destruction and the nation's number three killer. Sixty percent of adult children succumb to what they abhorred, be they genetically or socially infected, giving evidence to what Alcoholics Anonymous calls the *"cunning, baffling, and powerful"* nature of the illness.

As a child of an alcoholic, you need to pay close attention to your use of drugs and alcohol. You are more susceptible than the average person to developing addictions. If your drinking interferes with any aspect of your life—if you experience blackouts, guilt, sadness, or irrational anger while drinking—seek help. Alcoholism is a fatal disease.

Evidence suggests that if children of alcoholics don't become alcoholics themselves, they will often marry them (or other compulsive personalities). Dianna said: "My father was a nasty drunk. But I married a man just like him. Dave wasn't alcoholic when we got married. That took a couple years. But I should have suspected something when we were dating. Every time Dave picked me up for a date, he dropped off a six-pack for my dad."

Eating Disorders

Out of perceived need, some adult children practice bulimia, anorexia, overeating, or anything that abuses their bodies or damages their self-worth. These practices entrench individuals in familiar self-hatred and keep them from moving forward. Eating disorders, which are common in adult children, not only invite self-hatred, but also encourage control, guilt, anger, depression, and isolation.

Sandra, an adult child, speaks of recognizing her pattern in bulimia: "I was bulimic for fifteen years. The eating, the throwing up. My secret was the only thing that made me happy. But one day I realized it wasn't making me happy at all. Eating and throwing up were keeping me in the place my mother had kept me for years. I remembered her sneer as she drank and yelled at me. The tightness of her lips. Right then I knew bulimia was a substitute for my mother's voice screaming that I was bad and should be punished. I realized that if I continued to binge and purge, my mother would win. Her victory would be that I too would believe I was bad."

Violence

Violence was present in the childhoods of many adult children. The fear of abuse was as common as morning. Claudia Black, in *It Will Never Happen to Me!*, writes that the National Council on Alcoholism estimates that about 60 percent of the families receiving therapy for alcohol-related problems have been involved in domestic violence. Her personal research as a therapist indicates that 66 percent of the children from alcohol-controlled homes have either been abused or witnessed abuse of a family member.[2]

From her research on domestic violence, Black argues that witnessing abuse is as damaging as being battered. Whether witnessing or receiving, all children exposed to violence are at greater risk of perpetrating violence as adults (or even as children).

"When I was ten," Georgia said, "my father got mad because I wouldn't let my little brother play with me and my friends. I remember my father shouting at me and chasing me up the stairs, hitting me as I tried to run away. I remember crying in my room the rest of the evening. The next day, at school, I went into the bathroom and pulled my skirt way below my knees so that the handprint-shaped bruises wouldn't show. As a woman, I've been guilty of using my fists in anger, not with my children, but with my husband."

Abuse meant bruises, but it also meant fear. Frances recalls one of her memories: "When I was a child, I remember trying to block out my parents' fighting and cursing by lying in bed and humming. Sometimes I'd wrap the pillow around my head. At times I'd be awakened by my father banging his fist on the table. It terrified me! When I got older, I saved some money and bought a small radio and put it on my pillow."

In some homes, alcohol led to sexual abuse. Elizabeth remembers:

> One night my parents came back from the tavern drunk.
> They let a friend stay overnight on the couch because he was
> too drunk to walk home. In the middle of the night, I was
> awakened as the man removed my pajama bottoms. He was
> whispering that I was pretty and that he liked me. His words
> slurred and his hands touched me. I kept trying to get away.

To this day I don't understand why I was afraid to call out for help, but then I was afraid most of the time in my house.

In the darkness, the man kept threatening me. He warned me not to make noise. Then he tried to penetrate me. I got away and ran into the living room to hide. He came after me whispering my name and almost found me. I was cold and half naked and wanted to cry but was afraid that crying would reveal my hiding place. He kept crawling on his hands and knees reaching under things. Once he touched me but he didn't know it was me.

When he got to the other side of the room I crawled into my parents' room and tried to wake my mother. She pushed me away, drunk herself, and told me to go back to bed. I felt I had no choice but to crawl quietly back to my hiding place, but when I heard the man snoring on the couch, I crawled out of the room and slipped into bed with my sister. Today I get sick whenever anyone with liquor on his breath tries to kiss me.

Experiences like this jolt us and should force us to confront the hideous. Yet, having lived the hideous, many adult children end up inflicting physical, sexual, or verbal abuse on their own children. From a place of deep, deep wounding, some unhealed abuse victims become abusers.

Intimacy Problems

The fear of abandonment that entangled our childhoods now strangles our adult attempts at intimacy. This familiar fear, tying people to the past, causes children of alcoholics to pursue hopeless relationships and condemn themselves when the relationships fail. Adult children often love people who mistreat them, people who keep them feeling guilty or afraid or in whatever state their conditioned needs demand. "I only fall for the guy who two-times me or who has a gigantic macho ego and treats me like junk," Gretchen said. "The nice guys, the respectable kind, well, I couldn't care less about them." Or, confusing love with pity, adult children reach out to those they can rescue. Another technique is to create problems within a relationship, compelling loved ones to leave in frustration. Also, childhood perceptions of "I can't do anything right, I can't think straight, I can't trust anyone but myself, and I can't experience or express feelings" tend to interfere and damage relationships. Whatever the means, adult children frequently end up alone. The pattern repeats itself again and again, and you and I wonder why.

Not all failed relationships result from this need to be abandoned. Children learn how to be intimate by watching stable adults interact with one another. Children of alcoholics often witnessed fighting and blaming more than they saw caring and nurturing. Acknowledging the intimacy difficulties in his marriage, the son of an alcoholic father said: "Because of the way my parents treated each other, I thought that people primarily shouted at or avoided each other. It's hard for me to talk openly to my wife or to respect her as a person, since I never saw my parents do those things in their marriage."

"I want so badly to love and be loved in a normal relationship," Karen said. "I want to enjoy just living; but between what I do and what I never learned, I keep messing things up."

Karen speaks for many. Her desires are the desires of millions of adult children. So are her "mess-ups." To get well, children of alcoholics identify where they have been and what they need. Part I was written to help you with that process. You identified your present dysfunctions, went into your childhood environment, collected early memories, acknowledged your beliefs and the ways you tried to be lovable, identified your roles and their embellishments, and admitted how you may have kept yourself stuck and sabotaged sincere efforts to grow. You've come far, so rest for a while before beginning Part II—this process of healing can be draining. But as with surgery for the removal of a malignancy, you have to live through the procedure in order to get healthy.

After adult children begin to do that and sense healing, they are awed by how far they have come and how good they can feel. In Kathryn's words: "When I saw that I didn't have to look at myself through other people's eyes any longer, I was giddy. I felt free. I'm starting to balance care-giving and other behaviors, and I'm discovering a purely wonderful Kathryn."

Kathryn always was wonderful; getting well helps her know it. Part II offers you the same self-knowledge and a chance at the same self-healing that Kathryn is experiencing for yourself. It invites you to take an in-depth look at denial, anger, control, sadness, and forgiveness, and it will help empower your understanding of where you have been and who you are.

Part II

The Healing

Happy are those who know what sorrow means
for they will be given courage and comfort.
— Mt. 5:4

Chapter 8

Truth and Responsibility

I journey to the core of my being:
here is wholeness and gratitude.

"Then your light shall break forth like the dawn, and your wound shall quickly be healed" (Is. 58:8). Truth lives in the center of all things. It channels a being's purpose and potential, and it imparts wisdom, love, and peace. Truth is your inner light that waits to break forth like the dawn. This light of truth, this energy that illuminates meaning, is empowered through awareness.

The Chinese tell the story of an old man who owned a bony plow horse. One spring afternoon the horse ran away. The old man's friends, trying to console him, said, "We're so sorry about your horse, old man. What a misfortune you've had." But the old man said, "Bad news, good news—who knows?" A few days later the horse returned home leading a herd of wild horses. Again the friends came running. Filled with jubilation, they cried, "How wonderful!" But the old man whispered, "Good news, bad news—who knows?" Then the next day, when the farmer's son was trying to ride one of the new horses, the young man was thrown to the ground and broke both legs. The friends gasped. The old man stood still and said, "Bad news, good news—who knows?" And a short time later when the village went to war and all young men were drafted to fight, the farmer's son was excused because of two broken legs. Good news. Bad news. Who knows?

Take a moment to trace an important incident from your life, for example, the loss of a job or perhaps a chemical addiction. Applying this story's principles, concentrate on what happened and what you learned from the experience.

Enlightened awareness. The more you know, the more the line that separates good and bad begins to blur. In touch with truth, we accept life and self, and acceptance flowers wholeness.

Your journey towards wholeness began when you identified your childhood wounds. You faced the pain. Yes, life is difficult; that life is suffering is Buddha's First Noble Truth. But according to Jung, "The neurotic is ill because he is unconscious of his problems."[1] By walking into your pain and facing your problems, you are choosing to get well. When you disguise or ignore the pain, you force it to go underground and poison you from within.

When I'm avoiding pain, I retreat into what I call my "panic pocket." Trying to shelter myself, I crawl into a dark corner and immobilize myself with scary scenes from the past and scary predictions for the future.

When we acknowledge our pain, we live in the present. We transform pain's negative power into energy for healing. "The meaning and purpose of a problem," wrote Jung, "seem to lie not in its solution but in our working at it incessantly."[2] This working with problems (using their energy) is the life process.

To work with a problem, then, is to approach wholeness. And wholeness is a circumvolution, a turning toward the center, the light center, the truth that enables acceptance and the understanding of "good news, bad news—who knows?" Healing is to know that today is as it should be, that you already possess everything you need for the moment. It is a coming home to yourself in the awareness that all is well.

> *When the Shoe Fits*
> Ch'ui the draftsman
> Could draw more perfect circles freehand
> Than with a compass.
>
> His fingers brought forth
> Spontaneous forms from nowhere. His mind
> Was meanwhile free and without concern
> With what he was doing.
>
> No application was needed
> His mind was perfectly simple
> And knew no obstacle.

So, when the shoe fits
The foot is forgotten,
When the belt fits
The belly is forgotten,
When the heart is right
"For" and "against" are forgotten.

No drives, no compulsions,
No needs, no attractions:
Then your affairs
Are under control.
You are a free man.

Easy is right. Begin right
And you are easy.
Continue easy and you are right.
The right way to go easy
Is to forget the right way
And forget that the going is easy.

—Chuang Tzu (xix. 12)[3]

"All is well," freedom, is attainable through the healing process. You walk into your wounds, in touch with the healing power of your truth center. You can stand your pain. In fact, you can not only stand it, you can go beyond it for freedom and fullness. "No drives, no compulsions . . . You are a free man."

Somewhere in the middle of writing chapter 7, I experienced a healing and found freedom. I became a nonsmoker. For twenty-three years I smoked two packs of cigarettes a day. Cigarettes were my security, my happiness, my family. When I felt I couldn't rely on people, I believed cigarettes were reliable.

Then, while writing the first part of this book, insights surrounding my smoking habit surfaced into consciousness. My *inner child* added information. I did not plan this; I didn't want it to happen. I'd been a contented smoker who had dealt with other addictions, but had decided that smoking was different. I had resolved that one day I would have to quit for health reasons but had no intention of making "one day" now.

But something was happening as I wrote. Healing. Beyond my awareness, my truth center was drawing me to the knowledge that all was well, all was secure. Trust. Living in the now. It instilled the awareness that I possessed everything I needed for the moment. With that perception, I could lovingly release my smoking habit. I cried as I thanked it for helping me survive and then said good-bye. Somewhere in the middle of chapter 7 I experienced freedom. I am a nonsmoker. Hallelujah!

Similar "miracles" await everyone: wholeness is a birthright. Although each recovery is unique and unfolds within our personal process, self-realization is available to all. You know the way to heal you. I know the way to heal me. Aligning my power (my truth center) in the present, I focus on what I can do for me right now. Healing, then, springs effortlessly when I live in truth (that I deserve happiness or that I didn't cause anyone's alcoholism). When I take responsibility for my actions only and trust my ability to survive my healing process, I approach wholeness.

―――――――

The next six chapters encourage wholeness through responsibility. In Part I you entered the world of your present problems, your past experiences, and your behaviors. In Part II you may now address and moderate your feelings and defenses and the past and present behaviors they produce. Good news, bad news—who knows? These next chapters make use of the stages of death and dying identified by Elisabeth Kübler-Ross—denial, anger, bargaining, depression, and acceptance. Getting well is a dying and rebirth. It is the dying of mistaken perceptions and the rebirth of truth. It is replacing old beliefs with new life. Part II invites rebirth through the healing of illusions, injustice, control, and loss. This process prepares you for reaching wholeness through forgiveness. Wholeness means standing on your own feet, working your own inventory, and trusting reality.

"The more faithfully you listen to the voice within you, the better you will hear what is sounding outside," wrote Dag Hammarskjöld in *Markings*.[4] The "voice within you" is your truth center. "What is sounding outside" is reality.

―――――――

Chapter 9

The Healing of Illusions

---

*I am excited by life and filled
with life's abundant blessings.*

"Growing up, no one in the family talked about my father's drinking," Beth said. "I mean, NEVER. Twelve years after leaving home, I went into therapy because of anxiety and phobias. But it was a year after entering treatment before I mentioned my father's alcohol problem. When I did, I got so dizzy I started to pass out. I was the first person to 'go public' with Dad's drinking and I felt guilty."

Denial is alcoholism's mainstay: illusions permit the disorder to thrive. To make progress in your recovery, let chapter 9 first help you identify the vast collection of illusions you structured for survival as a child, and then help you restructure existing illusions.

We all use coping mechanisms in life. The degree to which we rely on them and are aware of them determines whether they are healthy or unhealthy for us. A healthy defense mechanism is balanced, meaning that you are aware of why and how you use it. Recognizing that I use a particular mechanism is essential, as is being aware of my true motive in using the particular defense. Does my coping mechanism help me solve the problem, or does it let me run away from it?

Used as a buffer, denial is a defense mechanism created to protect family members from the excesses that occur in an alcohol-controlled home. In your past, denial was necessary since escape kept you from "going crazy," and illusions kept you alive. But in adult life those early coping mechanisms are no longer appropriate: in fact, they create problems for you because they allow you to distort reality through rationalization, repression, projection, and fantasy. Study these forms of illusion; open yourself to identifying the positive and negative elements of each.

DEFENSE MECHANISMS

Rationalization

Rationalization, or providing justification for thoughts or actions, keeps some children of alcoholics sane. "Dad could be worse; he doesn't beat us," you may have said for protection. Perhaps you rationalized that what you experienced was exaggerated, or that all parents behaved as yours did. Maybe you intellectualized, a finely tuned way to rationalize without emotion. No matter their form, rationalizations offered immediate comfort, but they buried reality. They also buried fear and anger.

EXERCISE #25

Think of ways you may have rationalized as a child, and write down what you remember about the times you used this form of illusion.

Repression

Repression pushes negative thoughts from consciousness. It's a way of forgetting. The result is relief and that's fine, but repression stuffs feelings, and "stuffed" feelings fester. When you ignore what is real, you have little opportunity to be an authentic person. When you're authentic, you experience real feelings: you're sometimes angry, sometimes happy, sometimes sad. At all times you are you, who you are—not who you think other people want you to be.

As unhealed adults, adult children of alcoholics continue to stuff feelings with chemicals, smoking, overworking, excess sleep, television, overeating, casual sex.

EXERCISE #26

Do you stuff feelings? Think of how you stuffed feelings for protection as a child, and write down some examples that illustrate your use of this coping mechanism.

Projection

Projection shifts responsibility. It is a form of denial you possibly used for protection as a child. Unconsciously, you may have ascribed your painful feelings or actions to another. At times you may have done the same with wants and fantasies. "Grandma gets so angry when Mom drinks. Poor Grandma, she looks so sad. All she wants is to have Mom stop drinking," says a child, attributing his own feelings to his grandmother.

Projection hovers in the air of the alcoholic home like smoke in a smokehouse. Did you ever hear statements like these: "If it weren't for you children, I could leave your father right now," or "If you and your brother weren't so wild, I wouldn't have to drink to unwind," or "I don't have friends because of your mother's drinking. No one wants to come over anymore." Projection. A learned shifting of responsibility.

When we practice unbalanced (unconscious) projection as adults, reality is fuzzy. Truth blurs, and healthy problem solving is impossible until we take responsibility for our own feelings, actions, and fantasies. We have to admit that we're the ones who are sad before we can deal with our sadness and get better.

EXERCISE #27

Write down examples of how you used projection as a defense mechanism.

Fantasy

Fantasy protects some children of alcoholics from the pain of the real world. If you denied what was actually happening, you may have told yourself that you had the "nicest family on the block." Fantasy helped you believe that: "Mom couldn't come to the school play yesterday because she was sick with the flu." Living make-believe, you may have credited your family with possessing the warmth and stability you wanted it to have. Continuing that behavior into adult life can set you up for untold miseries because an altered sense of reality invites such excesses as chemical abuse and casual sex. By looking for a "high," you make a hollow thrill a substitute for "what is."

EXERCISE #28

If you sought comfort in fantasy, give an example illustrating how you used the defense mechanism as a child.

ALCOHOLISM WITHOUT ILLUSIONS

You wanted the alcoholic to stop drinking, you wanted peace in the home, yet your very system of denial, and that of others, perpetuated the chaos. All the ignoring and pretending allowed the alcoholic to continue in his illness. Many well-meaning people (including doctors, ministers, lawyers, and bosses) enabled the alcoholism. Not to imitate such modeling was probably impossible for you. But illusion weaves guilt, anger, fear, and sadness, all of which can cripple a child's spirit.

Those same cripplers frequently plague the adult lives of children of alcoholics. Larry, an adult child, commented: "I use denial so I don't have to face problems, but the resulting sadness is almost unbearable. I want to be loved, to see smiles, and to be touched by a friend, but I'm forever avoiding and running back within myself for protection. My loneliness is a perpetual, hollow aching."

In order to deal with alcoholism and the alcoholics in our lives without illusions, we must understand two facts: Alcoholism is a disease, and children do not cause or cure it.

Statistics concerning the disease from the American Medical Association are alarming. Alcohol and drug dependency are the primary illnesses of people in this country under age forty-five. Exclusive of pediatric and geriatric beds, 50 percent of all hospital admissions are related to chemical abuse.[1]

The ratio of male/female alcoholics is changing. More women are being ensnared by the disease. In the 1970s, ten men sought treatment for every woman who did, but we now find a ratio of only two or three males to every female. Statistics from the Betty Ford Center tell us that 87 percent of female alcoholics are cross-addicted to tranquilizers, 50 percent to sleeping pills, and 25 percent to other mood-altering drugs, a sizable number of which are prescribed by physicians.[2] When chemical addiction is denied and goes unrecognized as a disease (by you, by me, or by the medical community), danger lies in wait like quicksand. Alcoholism kills.

And alcoholism kills people at an earlier age than more traditional illnesses, according to the National Institute on Alcohol Abuse and Alcoholism. The institute reports that alcoholism steals an average of twenty-four years from a victim's natural life span. This is due to cirrhosis of the liver, traffic accidents, alcoholic hepatitis, dementia, and heart disease.

Just as no child causes a parent to be alcoholic, no parent consciously chooses to be one. At some point during an individual's drinking history, a change takes place, and he or she is alcoholic. It's as if an invisible line were crossed, one side of which is social drinking, the other side disease.

When that line is crossed, whether it's after seventy drinks or seven hundred (depending on personal chemistry), the person is sick. Reasons to drink vary. Men appear to drink to uphold an image, to be "one of the guys." Women tend to drink to block emotional discomfort. The reason doesn't matter; once that line is crossed, the disease is progressive and fatal. One way to further understand the illness and your relationship to it is to attend Al-Anon meetings. Al-Anon's principles help people who are, or have been, affected by an alcoholic.

The alcoholic is a good person who's controlled by an insidious disease. Consumed by rage and guilt, the alcoholic withers, helpless and confused. On your journey to wholeness, try to separate the pathology from the person so that you may understand that the alcoholic in your life was, or is, ill. The disease has hurt the alcoholic as much as it has hurt you. In your childhood alcoholic environment, family members were victims of victims. Understanding these facts can help you understand and deal with the alcoholic in your life.

EXERCISE #29

Recognizing that alcoholism is a disease, draw a shape to represent it. Once it's drawn, talk to the shape. Vent real emotions. Tell it how you feel. For example, you may say things like, "I hate what you did to my father," or "I despise how you killed my mother," or "I'm afraid of you because you made excitement a high for me so that I now create crisis after crisis in my life."

After you've finished, record what you feel towards this destructive illness. For example, you might write, "I feel anger towards alcoholism because it ruined my childhood," or "I feel sad because alcoholism robbed me of happy experiences I could have had with my mother," or "I'm excited by 'what is,' not by a crisis of my own invention."

Shape

EXERCISE #30

When you are ready to continue, take a deep breath, then exhale slowly. Relax, be aware of your breathing. Allow yourself to experience your surroundings, the air against your skin, the furnishings you see, any noises you hear. Relax and feel at peace. In a moment or two, allow your eyes to close, and then pretend you are a puppeteer. Imagine that you hold the strings attached to a puppet that looks just like you. You, the puppeteer, are exceedingly wise. You are aware of all things, especially reality, and you know that alcoholism is a disease. With your inner eyes, see the puppet meet the significant people in your life one by one. Moving the puppet, have it speak to the chosen people. Have the conversations deal with reality. Allow the puppet to explain how it has used denial in the past. Then have the puppet tell the important people in your life how it will live in reality in the present, how it will be energized by "what is," not by confusion. When you are ready to return to your ordinary surroundings, thank the puppet and say good-bye. Come back to the moment feeling refreshed and energized.

Chapter 10

The Healing of Injustice

---

*I am capable, confident, and secure
concerning all that I do.*

"My parents were alcoholics, and they never came to any of my school functions," Abby said. "I was always told 'maybe' or 'we'll see.' The last time I invited my mother to anything, I asked her to come to a Camp Fire Girls mother-daughter dinner. The meal was to be served at my girlfriend's house right next door. Mom had told me she would come, and I was so excited she was finally going to do something with me.

"That evening as the mothers arrived I watched the clock; Mom was late. I ran home to remind her and to tell her we were waiting for her. We had worked hard on the meal and were anxious to serve our mothers the finished product. When I walked in the door, Mom was at the kitchen table drinking beer. She said she was too tired to go. I begged and pleaded, but nothing changed. I returned to the party and told everyone she was sick, then went home because all I could do was cry.

"I quit the Camp Fire Girls and never again joined anything that involved parents."

THE ANGER WITHIN

This chapter, on the healing of injustice, addresses the anger that churns beneath the surface of most adult children of alcoholics. This anger is in reaction to what happened or what was missed in childhood.

All people feel angry at one time or another, of course. Anger is neither bad nor good; it is a feeling, not a behavior. In your home, anger was probably distorted, so as a child, you most likely denied and repressed anger for self-protection. Or perhaps you share Shannon's experience. "Anger was forbidden when I was growing up," said Shannon, the daughter of an alcoholic father and stepmother. "It was always made known that 'nice' girls didn't get angry, they smiled." Continued into adult life, repressed anger expresses itself through implosion or explosion.

- If it's directed inward (*implosion*), suppressed rage spurs various physical symptoms: headaches, digestive tract disorders, hypertension, depression. Imploded rage will eventually damage the internal organs.
- If it's directed outward (*explosion*), suppressed anger incinerates everyone and everything it encounters. Wild and tumultuous, misguided rage terrifies the self and others, and it confuses relationships. Out of pain, pain is inflicted.

Either expression is counterproductive. Unrecognized anger is dangerous. It is also ineffective for, without focus, anger's energy is scattered like breaking glass.

Normal behaviors that are taken to excess mask unidentified rage and keep adult children powerless: eating, drinking, shopping, gambling, or sexual activity. These behaviors become "instead ofs" that supplant healthy anger and damage the self and others. Hypochondria and anxiety attacks are other "instead ofs" for anger. And anger itself can be an "instead of" for sadness, since the root of anger is oftentimes loss.

Tremendous power boils within rage. Work to tap into that intense power, to identify and channel it creatively. When you are aware of the energy in your anger, you can direct it constructively to solve a problem, paint a house, or knead bread. In touch with your anger, you go further.

Cindy, an adult child and recovering alcoholic, relayed an incident from her life that demonstrates the consequences of imploded anger:

> Not too long ago, I went to visit my brother, Joe, in Wyoming. My brother and I are really close, probably because our parents are alcoholics, and through the years Joe and I had to stick together. The two of us sat at his kitchen table talking and drinking coffee that first night. Deep into

the conversation, Joe looked at me and said, "When I see you, Cindy, I know what Mother could be like if she weren't sick."

The comment startled me, and I began to cry. I thanked my brother and told him I was honored. But without my realizing it, the remark simmered. The next day I had a stiff neck. I felt restless and moody, and was tempted to drink. My irritability lasted for days, and I acted like a brat experiencing an occasional headache and sore throat.

A week or so later, after getting back home, I went to my Adult Children of Alcoholics discussion group. The meeting that night was on resentment. I drank a cup of coffee and listened to others talk about dealing with anger. But as I listened, I started to feel strange. My jaw muscles tightened, my neck felt hot. Then it surfaced. Anger. Raw imploded anger. Trusting the group, I allowed my feelings to jet upward. As loving as my brother's comment had been, I'd reacted to the statement with self-pity and anger. The comment had sparked a "poor me" response. Because my mother was an alcoholic, I had to learn about life by myself. Oh, poor me. I had to learn the hard way with lots of mistakes, and that made me angry. Since I'm an alcoholic I have to pay close attention to "poor me," for "poor me" can quickly become "pour me" a drink.

I had carried that wagonload of anger for ten days. And what did it get me? A stiff neck, a sore throat, the desire to drink, and a lousy disposition. Nasty baggage. But at the Adult Children meeting, when I finally acknowledged and released the feelings, I found peace. When I let the anger out, my whole body relaxed. My perspective changed and I could look at the situation and say, "Okay, so my mom was drunk and couldn't help me much when I was growing up. Well, I've become a strong woman on my own in spite of that, and I'm proud of it."

Due to the early habit of repressing feelings, children of alcoholics may have a difficult time recognizing their anger. The process can seem frightening. Remember Pietra? To her, as a child, anger meant that terrible things were happening. As an adult, Pietra associates anger with terror and is unwilling to experience her anger. Reacting to her fear, she manacles her energy and finds herself agitating and procrastinating.

People who fear that others won't like them if they express anger will also have trouble identifying the emotion. The perception is accurate: some people don't like seeing healthy anger expressed. But those are people who are afraid of anger themselves.

RECOGNIZING YOUR RAGE

Before you begin the exercise that follows, be prepared to encounter difficulties and fear. As mentioned, recognizing your rage contradicts years of learned behavior. You may feel guilty or that you're a bad person. Such reactions accompany change. If you discover painful feelings, pat yourself on the back. Distress indicates that you are counteracting previous, harmful messages. Your reactions show how deeply entrenched your early behaviors have become. Remind yourself of that if the work seems overpowering.

If you feel faint, affirm yourself in the present by focusing on a nearby object. Don't worry. The fear of rage can cause light-headedness. Feeling dizzy is a common reaction.

Many adult children scare themselves by thinking they won't be able to control the power of their rage, that it may overwhelm them. That reaction is also normal in people accustomed to stuffing anger. If that is your experience, ask someone you trust to sit with you while you work an exercise. Your friend can offer encouragement, saying things like, "Good for you. You're clear and strong in your anger. You can stand your anger. Go with it. Experience it. Good work."

Be careful to stay with the anger. Some may feel the need to cry, but tears only dilute anger's power. For this exercise, try to remain in your anger as long as possible.

When you are ready, use any of the following four suggestions to get in touch with your anger. These suggestions unlock rage through large muscle involvement and inner sound release. The safe expression of anger allows you to feel its power, almost to scoop it out and hold it in your hands. To deny your anger is to deny your strength. Anger is healthy, usable energy.

The purpose of the following exercise is to tap into the power of your anger, but your tapping process may require more structure than the workbook offers. If you have excessive difficulty identifying and channeling your anger, or if you fear that your rage is so intense you might injure yourself or another, get professional counseling. Many excellent workshops on dealing with anger are available throughout the country. "Fair Fight Training" is one. Call your Mental Health Association to locate a program that can help you. Or, if you like, make an appointment with a therapist and explain that you want help with anger. Trust yourself and get the protections you need.

EXERCISE #31

1. Find a large towel. Twist the towel, then bite into it, working your jaw and neck muscles. As you bite, release your constrained energy through sound. Growl or scream "No!" Emitting sound is important. If this is difficult for you, go into the bathroom and turn on the shower. The water's noise will camouflage your sounds.

2. Anger may be experienced through exertion. Allow yourself to feel your anger's power by swimming or bicycling. Another physical way to unlock anger is to walk around and stamp your feet. If you can, make sounds to equal the intensity of the physical action.

3. Another way to release repressed anger is to sit in your car and yell as loudly as you can. Find a back road, park the car, and scream with all your might. Feel the surging energy. Have a friend accompany you.

4. Go to your room and have a tantrum. Clear off your bed, then lie across it, and pound the mattress with your fists and legs. Don't just bat or swat. This is your opportunity to express significant levels of rage. Be aggressive and find your power.

Once you have felt the power in your anger, take time to thank yourself for acknowledging this potent gift. You are in touch with your anger and its strength. You may now use this vital energy to solve problems or be creative. Identifying your anger allows you to act rather than to react, to be victor rather than victim. When I'm angry, I'd much rather use the energy to wallpaper a room than to sit with a headache all day.

Assertive language clarifies feelings and is an important tool when you work to identify your anger. Ask for what you need, especially when your rights are denied: "I feel angry when I talk to you and you read the paper. I need your attention," or "I feel angry when you don't tell me what's bothering you and I have to 'read your mind' to discover the problem." Trust yourself and stress your feelings. Assertive language has clean edges. No games are played; no one is attacked. You define how you feel and what you want without hurting yourself or another.

Whether you use one of my four suggestions or try another method (perhaps running, talking, or writing), transforming your anger heals the wounds that resulted from perceived childhood injustice. As you acknowledge and experience clean anger, you are freed to grow closer to others and to touch your own authenticity. Thomas Merton wrote, "Your life is shaped by the end you live for. You are made in the image of what you desire."[1] When you desire wholeness, you become wholeness. Going into your anger, you discover the power of who you are.

EXERCISE #32

The Healing Dance

Take a deep breath and recall the energy you discovered through the previous anger exercises. If you like, choose a piece of music that expresses the intensity of your anger. As you play the record or tape, close your eyes and listen for a moment. When you are ready, begin to move to the music. Experience your anger's positive energy through the music and throughout your body. The energy, not the anger, propels your arms, your legs, your torso, your head. Healing energy surges through your bones, through your muscles, through every cell in your body. Move and become the positive power you discovered in your anger. Dance. Free your entire being. This is your power, the power you imprisoned in your denied anger. As you move with the music, see the energy transform into healing light. See the light radiate from your body outward. Experience the light. Notice that the source of the light is the core of your being. Dance the awareness. You are alive in the light, alive in the center of your own goodness. Dance and celebrate the power of who you are.

Chapter 11

The Healing of Control

I am worthwhile and lovable.

Children who learn that their parents cannot be trusted tend to rely on themselves almost totally. But self-reliance is one thing; distrust is another. This kind of childhood wariness eventually sculpts adults who need to feel "in charge" of their well-being at all times. These individuals cannot trust others with their feelings, tasks, property, safety. They are compelled to direct their entire world. They need to maintain rigid control.

This chapter invites adult children of alcoholics to trace their past and present control behavior, and to set up a program to balance it.

The chaos that many children of alcoholics experience in childhood demands regimentation to achieve stability. The daughter of an alcoholic father said, "Because everything was crazy around our house, I set pretty narrow rules for myself for security. One was that I'd meet friends at their houses, not mine. Another was that I'd try not to talk to my father after seven o'clock at night." In innocence these children balance, as if on wire, in desperate attempts to simulate normalcy: each step is practiced, each step is placed with care. Cozy bungalows deceive outsiders, for the rooms inside are rigged with land mines. Survival in an alcoholic home is serious business.

TRYING TO CONTROL

Amidst such confusion, self-defense becomes absolute. Many children of alcoholics cling to survival by controlling their bodies, minds, and other people. Taking care of your body is healthy, so is disciplining your mind. Danger occurs when those practices are carried to the extreme or are used for negative purposes.

Controlling Your Body

Trouble looms when children of alcoholics control their bodies with bulimia, anorexia, overeating, or compulsive exercise, and try to use these excesses to improve their appearance, get attention, or gain emotional comfort. Amy, the thirty-year-old daughter of an alcoholic father, spoke of her bulimia. "Because life was so totally out-of-control in my family when I was a teenager, I was ecstatic when I discovered I could control my weight with eating and purging, and remember saying to myself, 'Hey, this is terrific!' But what began as control over my body image has progessed into an addictive habit that I'm having trouble living with. I feel so guilty now."

Controlling Your Mind

Trouble also looms when children of alcoholics use mental powers for negative reasons—to separate themselves from others, for example, or to manipulate people.

Donna commented on *controlling to separate*: "When I was a child, I was afraid of everybody. As I went through school, though, I discovered I was an excellent student and could use that gift to make myself different from others so they'd leave me alone. Playing 'head of the class' allowed me to control who'd come near me—and that usually meant no one."

Stuart commented on *controlling to manipulate*: "My mother needed to be powerful. She tried to control me by ordering me around and telling me what to do. When I was young I thought she was too strong for me, but I now see that I controlled her very subtly—passive aggression I think it's called. Mother was an art teacher. When she found out that I could paint, she sat me in a chair and gave me paints and paper. That was most unusual. I painted a picture of a bus over a bridge which she immediately had matted and framed. Then she entered the painting in an art contest. The picture won first place, and one of the judges took me aside to interview me for the radio. 'Why did you paint the picture?' he asked. 'Because my mother made me,' I answered. Mother was furious with me, and that was the last picture I ever painted. What sabotage."

Controlling Others

Controlling others seemed necessary for survival. "I wanted my mother to pay attention to me," Rosemary said, "but she was absorbed in what my father was doing, his drinking up our money and losing his job. The only time she noticed me was when I was sick. She was so good to me then, bringing tea and toast up to my room. Looking back on it, I realize I controlled my mother's attention in those days with a multitude of illnesses. To this day, when I want attention, I get sick."

In order to protect the fragile inner self, many children of alcoholics talk of having had to put on "masks": controlling with disguises. "The 'con' was the thing," Roy said. "And I remember the first time I used it. My uncle, an alcoholic, lived with us when I was growing up. He was always screaming at me. One day he was yelling and had me pinned against the stairs so I couldn't get away. That was the first time I 'put on a mask.' I turned off my ears and hid behind a face that pretended to listen. Behind my mask I knew I was safe. It was the only way I felt I could beat him."

The more alcohol controls their lives, the more children of alcoholics are obsessed by a need to control the areas they can influence—and with any method possible.

EXERCISE #33

If you controlled out of the need for self-protection or to manipulate others as a child, list the areas you controlled and how you controlled them.

LETTING GO

The compulsive need to control the uncontrollable threatens serenity and serendipity. It is important that you accept the fact that you are powerless over many events and most people; to demand that they change is to guarantee pain. The harder you push, the more you encounter resistance and antagonism. Needing to control, you end up controlled. Rigid tools honed in childhood for self-defense now cut deep wounds of frustration and loneliness. To recover, you need to let go.

Letting go begins with Al-Anon's first step: "We admitted we were powerless over alcohol—that our lives had become unmanageable." Yes, you were, and are, powerless over alcohol; but you are also powerless over people and other aspects of life you may try to control out of a need for security.

Letting go of the uncontrollable is a way to find peace. To let go is to live in the present. Ken Keyes, Jr., in his valuable *Handbook to Higher Consciousness*, wrote this:

> The past
>   is dead
> The future
>   is imaginary
> Happiness
>   can only be
> in the Eternal
> Now
> Moment.[1]

Focus on the moment, although living in the moment, the "now," is difficult. We forever stare over our shoulders at the past, or squint into the distance to find the future. We know that both waste energy, but *knowing* seldom makes *doing* come easier.

All happiness is right here, right now. Yet how often we miss the fullness of the moment. For example, in my garden I worry over whether or not the tomatoes will ripen, and I worry over whether or not the rabbits will eat the kohlrabi, as they did last year. Think of all the happiness I skip over when I worry. "Gardening is an active participation in the deepest mysteries of the universe," according to Thomas Berry.[2] I overlook countless "mysteries of the universe" when I focus on the past or the future and disregard the present. Yet when I savor the "now," I find peace.

You can apply Step One from Al-Anon to all control issues. So often, when we decide that another person needs to be shown how to change, we attempt to "right" his perceived "wrongs" by setting up *shoulds* and *should nots.* But control becomes mistreatment. Recognizing the pattern requires the mature realization that you can only work on yourself, not another. Tolstoy described the process when he wrote, "I sit on a man's back, choking him and making him carry me, and yet I assure myself and others that I am very sorry for him and wish to ease his lot by all possible means—except by getting off his back."

EXERCISE #34

Write down the names of people you suspect you may be choking:

ACCEPTING REALITY

To further our wholeness, we must release our death grips, which strangle others' freedoms and our own personal power. We have no right to change others, only to change ourselves. Yet the paradox is, when we let go of "fixing" others and work to change ourselves, our outward conditions miraculously improve. As Daniel, an adult child, said: "The strangest thing happened. I made some personal changes and everyone around me seemed to get better."

Like people damming up a river, many of us, out of an imagined need for self-protection, decided to design and control the uncontrollable in our lives. And the outcome of this willfulness? Fear. Guilt. Frustration. Loneliness. To achieve wholeness, we must unblock the river through surrender.

God grant me the
Serenity to accept the things I cannot change;
Courage to change the things I can; and
Wisdom to know the difference.

Reinhold Niebuhr's "Serenity Prayer" distills the essence of this chapter's aspirations. You and I can find peace through surrender—neither giving up nor giving in, but by gently accepting reality. Acknowledging our present conditions, ourselves, and those around us, we move from anger to forgiveness, from anxiety to informed acquiescence. By accepting the *uncontrollable*, we free ourselves to channel energy toward the *controllable*. When you and I allow people and situations to be as they are, we are free to mold what can be changed—our thoughts, our decisions, and our actions.

You literally become what you think, so positive thought control is important. When you believe you're strong, you become strong. When you believe you're a good problem solver, you solve problems well. Thoughts are things, as real as a bottle of liquor or a child's innocence. Your thoughts have made you who you are, have arranged your life without one incident of chance. And your positive thoughts can help you heal.

EXERCISE #35

If you would like, write out some negative thoughts you now hold. Then rewrite each thought so that it becomes positive.

> **Example**
> **Negative thought:** *Because finances are tight and I can't afford to have the house painted, painting it myself will eat up all my free time this summer.*
> **Positive thought:** *Painting the house this summer will allow me to be outdoors, to get good exercise, and to achieve a strong sense of accomplishment.*

Negative thought

Positive thought

Once we grasp this powerful idea, our vocabulary changes. We discard negative words and statements, and life begins to flourish under this positive influence. Our choice of words can change our thoughts; our thoughts can change our lives.

Healing occurs when we live in the moment, stop trying to control the uncontrollable, and begin to change what we do have power over: our thoughts, our decisions, and our actions. Our only real problem in life is to decide how we choose to control it.

EXERCISE #36

Part 1

Below, list five areas you have the power to control: your weight, for example, or your career choice. Be aware that you cannot control others and that it is not your responsibility to do so.

1.

2.

3.

4.

5.

Part 2

Next, list five areas you cannot control (your spouse, for instance, or your employer), and describe the frustrations that result when you try to control them.

1.

2.

3.

4.

5.

Part 3

Finally, record ways you will change your thoughts, your decisions, your actions. To help you, I offer some examples from my life.

Thoughts

> **Example:** *I will think of every person as a loving person trying to do his or her best in life.*

Decisions

> **Example:** *I will not tell my children what to do.*

Actions

> **Example:** *I will give my children information, then allow them to make their own choices.*

———————

You and I have the power to be as small as our most restricting need or as great as our most liberating dream. How and what we attempt to control directs the outcome. We accept the things we cannot change. With courage we change our thoughts, our decisions, and our actions so that we may find wholeness and peace. And we pray for the wisdom to know when to accept and when to change. Simple, but not easy, so be accepting of yourself while you learn.

———————

Chapter 12

The Healing of Loss

Everything I need I possess in this moment.

Last night I forgot to put the dinner in the oven. The chicken was prepared, the oven was on. But the cookie sheet of "Shake and Bake" legs, thighs, and wings got sidelined on the kitchen counter. I don't drink or use drugs, and I hope I'm not senile. What I do, and did yesterday, is stuff feelings.

My parents recently gave me a box that contained the letters I had written home during college. I sat up one night and read the two hundred letters. I saw my handwriting change as my experience broadened. The Kennedy assassination and the great New England blackout were chronicled. But I also found descriptions of dates with my first husband, and college friends I had pushed aside. Indelible fear and "people-pleasing" inked every page. Finishing the letters, I felt sadness swell within me like bruised tissue. I recognized how, on some level, I had sabotaged important relationships, how I had married a controlling individual with whom I was terrified of being myself.

I now know it would have been impossible for me to have married another type of personality at that time. Insecurity was the familiar, my payoff, a state I needed to maintain. On a primordial level, the relationship was exciting but doomed.

I dragged under the weight of the sadness of this journey into the past. I wanted to grieve for the girl who had spent so many years afraid, who had pushed people away, who had been unable to recognize her unhealthy subconscious needs, and who had thus entered into a difficult marriage. But I didn't grieve—I stuffed. I stuffed the sadness and forgot to put the dinner in the oven. Later that night, I forgot to make the coffee I'd promised to bring to the PTA meeting. Stuffing emotions requires enormous energy— like trying to cap an erupting Mount St. Helens with a manhole cover.

GRIEVING YOUR LOSSES

Allow this chapter to help you face the immense sadness that surrounds your memories of parents who couldn't be present and dreams that couldn't be fulfilled. Adult children need to let down their protective defenses, experience their losses, and cry. When they accept their vulnerability, they can expel their grief through tears and cleanse their wounds in preparation for healing. When they avoid that grief, they bend under the burden of unresolved sadness.

Ignoring feelings has many negative results; absentmindedness is insignificant by comparison. Consider bitterness, for example. Although it's a defense against loss, bitterness can harden spirits and distance adult children from others. Or loneliness. To protect themselves from projected blows, many adult children either jump ahead at the first attack or withdraw behind walls and masks. Whether they're attacking or withdrawing, they end up alone.

Sometimes I sense tears within myself, but fearing the tears might smother me, I refuse to release them. Yet my unexpressed tears become brine for self-pity, a murky solution that keeps me stuck. Tiffany, an adult child of alcoholic parents, spoke of her self-pity: "When I was little my dad gave me a hard time whenever I felt bad. He'd shake his head and tell me to stop feeling sorry for myself. I soon learned I couldn't be sad in our house. I had to hide the feeling. To this day I have trouble dealing with sadness. I keep hearing my dad's words and keep stuffing my sadness. Than I stew and feel sorry for myself and end up compulsively eating junk food. That's been my pattern for years." When I'm into self-pity, I blame everyone but myself for my problems, and I tell myself I'm helpless. Self-pity is my grown-up way of whining.

Ignoring sadness also invites depression, the root of which is oftentimes loss. When loss turns anger inward, it has the potential, like the parasite it resembles, to destroy. Concerning depression, Rory, an adult child, said: "My mother died when I was five years of age. At some point after that I decided not to deal with my sadness and anger. I denied their existence. To ignore those feelings I had to ignore all feelings, including happy ones. My decision eventually led to depression. It cost me a first marriage, threatened a second one, and separated me from my children. I finally sought professional help when I began to entertain thoughts of suicide."

Adult children must surface their unresolved losses and devise ways to grieve and further their healing. Admittedly, this is difficult: we are the most protected where we are the most vulnerable. But if we choose to evade the pain, we must recognize that we're choosing to allow bitterness, self-pity, and depression to continue crippling our relationships and threatening our wholeness. We have a choice—to acknowledge and integrate loss or to run away.

> *Flight from the Shadow*
> There was a man who was so disturbed by the sight of his own shadow and so displeased with his own footsteps that he determined to get rid of both. The method he hit upon was to run away from them.
>
> So he got up and ran. But every time he put his foot down there was another step, while his shadow kept up with him without the slightest difficulty.
>
> He attributed his failure to the fact that he was not running fast enough. So he ran faster and faster, without stopping, until he finally dropped dead.
>
> He failed to realize that if he merely stepped into the shade, his shadow would vanish, and if he sat down and stayed still, there would be no more footsteps.
>
> —Chuang Tzu (xxxi)[1]

Like footsteps or a shadow, losses do not go away. Recovery asks that they be acknowledged and assimilated.

Visualize yourself as a box of crayons, with each crayon representing some issue in your life. Every crayon, every issue, is real and occupies a certain amount of space in the box. Imagine that the red crayons are healthy, healed issues, issues that you have acknowledged and assimilated. They color pictures that are vibrant and alive. The blue crayons are unhealed issues: the pictures they color are dark and scary. Every blue crayon in the box takes up a space that could house a red crayon. Dealing with issues, through anger or grief or whatever is needed, allows you to transform a blue crayon into a red one. As your process evolves, you become a container of bright, vital, healthy energy—a box of red crayons, multihued and powerful.

EXERCISE #37

Part 1

Take a healing breath, hold it, then exhale slowly. As you continue to breathe, be aware of the breath in and out, and follow the breath at your nostrils. When you feel relaxed, contact your inner child for assistance. Remember, your inner child is the part of you that's been present since birth and is aware of your needs and motivations. The child loves you, wants you to survive, and can be enlisted to help further your well-being.

Part 2

When you are ready, invite your inner child to assist you with the following exercise, which asks you to remember what you wanted from life (needs and daydreams) when you were six, twelve, and seventeen years old—three significant ages in a child's life. If you cannot remember and don't want to contact your inner child, you may guess or make something up.

Age six

Age twelve

Age seventeen

Part 3

Next, identify which of those needs and wants were satisfied and which were not.

Age six

What I got

What I didn't get

Age twelve

What I got

What I didn't get

Age seventeen

What I got

What I didn't get

Part 4

Ask your inner child to tell you what now needs to be dealt with and grieved over. Write the child's responses in the space below. For example, my inner child tells me that I need to grieve over the emptiness I feel because of the limited relationship I've had with my mother.

Areas to be grieved

Part 5

To heal your sadness, ask your inner child to reveal the best way to grieve for each issue. The program will encompass three areas:

1. How you will think about the issue (positive focus).

2. How you will feel about the issue (positive focus).

3. What specific thing(s) you will do to achieve your goals.

Together you and your inner child can set up a program that best meets your need to grieve. If you feel uncomfortable with the exercise, know you can come back to it at another time.

Example
I asked my inner child to tell me the most healing way to grieve for the loss I felt concerning my mother. My inner child responded that healing would be furthered through music. When she offered that suggestion, I knew it was right. I could feel the "a-ha" sensation (like fitting the right peg into the correct slot); music has always soothed me, so I accepted the suggestion and refined it. I named a particular piece of music, a piece I associated with strength, and decided I would listen to it once a week, using the music to fill empty spaces I still felt because of my loss. So I completed the list this way:

1. *I will know the music is filling my emptiness.*
2. *I will feel peaceful.*
3. *Once a week I will listen to "Pachelbel's Canon" performed by harpist Kim Robertson on her* Water Spirit *tape.*

Your suggestions
When you are ready, ask your inner child for suggestions on the best way to grieve and heal, then record and implement the suggestions. Thank your inner child for the loving gifts.

1. How I will think about the issue (positive focus).

2. How I will feel about the issue (positive focus).

3. What specific thing(s) I will do to to achieve my goals.

EXERCISE #38

Another exercise you might find helpful is to write a sentence or paragraph that states what you feel now. Then keep writing until you find the phrase that makes you cry. After identifying your grief statement, draw a line under it and then jot down whatever comes to mind.

Example
Grief statement
Dad, because you had to withdraw to protect yourself from what was going on in our family, I feel I lost you to the disease, too. I missed you when I was little **and I miss you now.**

What came to my mind
- *sadness that seems unending*
- *alone, no father or mother*
- *a wonderful relationship that was never allowed to be*
- *poor Dad, how sad you must feel*
- *alcoholism is deadly*

Your grief statement
If you would like, write down your grief statement and your related thoughts.

What came to mind

Once you have written out a grief statement, you may return to work with it as often as you'd like. In the future you might write other statements, depending on what remains to be grieved over. You may choose to resolve your grief by deciding what you want to think, feel, and do about it, or by using one of the other exercises in this chapter.

No matter how you choose to resolve your grief, you can't let go of it until you experience it. You must track it down until it is finally dissipated and you are whole.

TECHNIQUES FOR SELF-KNOWLEDGE

Another way to work through loss is to strengthen self-knowledge. Empty spaces in your life may be filled with parts of yourself. You are wisdom. You are love. A clear sense of who you are makes you aware that you already possess what is missing or is wanted.

There is no one way to develop that "clear sense" of who you are and what you possess. I have offered some techniques that I use, but you will discover others through readings and/or your own imagination.

Keep a Journal

Keeping a journal is an important tool for me. In a journal you can record your deepest thoughts and feelings to document the growth process. Be free and spontaneous in your journal. Write down experiences, emotions, daydreams, inspirations, desires—anything that uncovers who you are.

Use your journal as a daily inventory to identify progress or to highlight areas that need attention. Your journal is also the place to record your needs and how you can meet them. Journals are wonderful. You discover who you are, layer upon layer, like petals of the lotus.

In order to be open in your journal, keep it away from the eyes of others. Candor requires security. Since the journal is just for your eyes, it needn't be a "coffee table" book or be "perfect." Draw, sketch, and doodle as you write. Be free and inventive.

Start a Dream Diary

Begin a dream diary. Dreams are powerful answers from the subconscious. The Talmud says that "a dream not understood is like a letter unopened." Dreams are rich sources of knowledge that complete your waking life. They offer creative solutions to problems. By symbolically dramatizing difficulties and resolutions, dreams keep poking you until you pay attention and take care of the problems. Value your dreams; they are insights from you to you.

Share Your Story

Your sense of self is also strengthened when you assist the healing of another adult child. Tell your story—"what happened, and what you are like now"—so that another may get well. Helping another adult child is an important recovery tool. As you share your feelings and history, the power of the past is weakened. Saying aloud where you have been clarifies the facts and confirms present choices. The extended hand returns blessed.

Identify Your Feelings

One of the most valuable techniques for self-knowledge is to identify your feelings daily. If you know what you're feeling, you can deal with the emotion immediately, which then allows you to settle negative ones and savor positive ones in the process of making room for bright red crayons.

EXERCISE #39

If self-knowledge feels like a tool that can help you deal with loss, write down four ways you will begin, or further, your self-awareness.

1.

2.

3.

4.

———————————

To resolve sadness is painful, yes. Not to resolve it is more painful because a buried loss paralyzes. We never bury (deny) anything "dead." Ignored issues are alive, and they can return to haunt us through a myriad of physical and emotional discomforts. We have to identify our losses and grieve over them, sometimes again and again. Our losses are important and can have deep roots. Releasing tears, however, makes room for new life.

You may discover that you have to return to the exercises four or five times, and that's all right. Be patient with your needs. Expecting to read the chapter once and feel better is unreasonable. Give yourself permission to be broken for a while, then go on.

———————————

Chapter 13

To Forgive Is to Heal

*I am at peace with all people
at all times, including myself.*

To forgive is to heal. That's a catchy title, but even if it's possible, it sounds absurd. Forgiving (letting someone off the hook?) seems unnatural. After an injury, I want to soothe my wounds and attack the attacker. Platitudes like "turn the other cheek" sit on the tongue like stale bread. Take a moment and get angry if you'd like. Stomp around and let the anger out. Scream things like, "After all that happened, I have to forgive? No way. That's not fair. I'm no Mahatma Gandhi or Mother Teresa. I'm simple, not saintly."

If you feel angry, that's fine. Remember that anger's okay. You won't be sent to your room in this workbook for releasing usable energy. Get in touch with your real self, and if that self is angry, terrific. Anger's not a behavior to be judged, it's a feeling. I've spent enough years being everything but real, so when I finally feel authentic I commend myself. If you want to get mad, get mad. But come back and read on: there *is* something to forgiveness.

Forgiveness restores harmony. It is a healthy sort of selfishness that has nothing to do with another person. Adult children restore harmony not to "let someone off the hook" but to quiet their insides so they can get on with life.

Forgive is a verb, something you do. On the journey from injury to serenity, forgiving is the act of consciously deciding to let go and become something more than you have been. To forgive is to decide to come home to yourself in peace.

I hope that the roadways to forgiveness were smoothed through previous chapters. You acknowledged the past, recognized reality, identified your anger, mourned your losses, and relinquished control. Prior chapters should have helped prepare for the forgiving process, and forgiveness is worth the preparation. As much as you want to fight it, forgiving releases you from the past and frees you to thrive in the present. It is a conscious decision to let go and go on.

Because it is a "conscious decision," you control the process. No one forces you to forgive, and the person being forgiven needn't cooperate. Forgiveness relies solely on the forgiver. You can decide to do nothing and remain in misery, or you can decide to forgive and go on.

Sometimes adult children feel they can't forgive because of the depth of a wound or its newness. That's normal. But not to forgive grafts you to the past like a flowering branch to a disfigured tree. Others won't forgive out of pride or the need for revenge. But do you want to get even or get well? Pride and revenge halt the healing; they boomerang to deepen the wound by reaffirming the old tapes that say you are bad or unlovable.

I don't know about you, but I'm done with that garbage. I'm "sick and tired of being sick and tired." I want to get on with my life, and if that means forgiving, I'll forgive.

I remember first making a conscious decision to forgive a few years ago. I had no idea what I was doing. I was sitting in the family room of my house on Christmas Eve day. The only insight I had was that I was miserable. A few weeks before that, my mother had said something to me while she'd been drinking, and I had reacted with anger. Since then I'd been depressed and moody. But that day, in the family room, I decided I'd had enough. I remember thinking something like this: "I can't afford to give any more energy to this problem; it's draining me. I let go of what you said, Mother, and how I reacted, so that *I can feel better*. From now on, whenever I see or think of you, I will imagine love for you—for both of our sakes. This incident and all past incidents are over." Immediately I felt relief.

My mother hadn't done anything to make me feel better. I didn't use pious or profound words. Relief came once I decided to let go for inner peace.

EXERCISE #40

How to Forgive

If you would like to restore inner harmony, try using this step-by-step procedure to help you forgive. Know that you may use it as is or adapt it to suit your needs.

1. Take a pencil and your workbook to a comfortable place where you'll be uninterrupted. Sit quietly for a few minutes.

2. When you feel relaxed, complete the following statement.
   TODAY, FOR MY OWN WELL-BEING,
   I CHOOSE TO FORGIVE THESE PEOPLE:

   Then read the statement out loud.

3. Next, complete the following:
   TODAY, FOR MY OWN WELL-BEING,
   I CHOOSE TO FORGIVE THESE THINGS
   THAT WERE DONE TO ME:

   Please read what you've written out loud.

4. Now read what follows aloud:
   I LET GO OF THE ABOVE INCIDENTS, AND MY REAC-
   TION TO THEM, AND I WISH THE PEOPLE I HAVE
   NAMED SINCERE GOODWILL. IF AN INDIVIDUAL IS
   DECEASED, I WISH HIM OR HER ETERNAL PEACE. IN
   DOING SO, I RELEASE MYSELF FROM THE PAST AND ITS
   PAIN. THE PEOPLE AND INCIDENTS I HAVE FORGIVEN
   NO LONGER HAVE POWER OVER ME.[1]

TO FORGIVE IS TO HEAL

Gerald G. Jampolsky, M.D., in *Love Is Letting Go of Fear*, wrote:

> The unforgiving mind, contrasted with the forgiving mind,
> is confused, afraid and full of fear. It is certain of the
> interpretation it places on its perceptions of others. It is
> certain of the justification of its anger and the correctness of
> its condemning judgment. The unforgiving mind rigidly sees
> the past and future as the same and is resistant to change. It
> does not want the future to be different from the past. The
> unforgiving mind sees itself as innocent and others as guilty.
> It thrives on conflict and on being right, and it sees inner
> peace as its enemy. It perceives everything as separate.[2]

Since thoughts are things, when you believe you're separate, you become separate. Not to forgive isolates you through judgment and self-righteousness. Not to forgive fosters dysfunction. Forgiveness, however, unifies and heals. When you forgive, you let go of separateness, anger, guilt, loss, and other persistent tormentors. Freeing others, you free yourself.

Children of alcoholics made decisions and judgments on the basis of what they knew as children, but their knowledge was incomplete. In ignorance and for self-protection, these children cursed family members who were being consumed by a disease. Doing so, they injured themselves with their own screams.

Once you decide to forgive, the difficult part is over. You are only asked to make the decision and to say the words. A power greater than you releases the healing. Some call that power the good. Others, like myself, call it God. Regardless of the name, it is a power greater than human power.

A few adult children have trouble accepting the concept of God or a "Higher Power." "Someone just mentions the word 'God' and I start to run," one of my sisters said recently. "But wanting to feel better, I'm trying to be open. One of the men in my adult children group is helping me. He said that if I keep coming to the meetings I'll eventually understand. 'If you can't make it, fake it. Acting *as if* is a way to get there,' were his words. I'm trusting him because I see in him what I want. For now I'm using the energy of the group as my Higher Power."

With patience and through surrender, healing progresses, and a new, profound, unintended, uninvited awareness sets in. This unexpected gift is the realization that you are more because of where you have been. The knowledge arrives with time (sometimes a very long time) and without fanfare. Blessed by this healing realization, you reach a point where you are able to say, "I forgive you for hurting me, because the pain brought wisdom and growth. I am more because of what happened, therefore, I am grateful."

With the gift of this wisdom, adult children soar beyond their own imaginings. No longer fearing the past, they enter it and transform their demons into opportunities. When adult children are unafraid of the pain of the past, they take risks and involve themselves in life. Wisdom encourages involvement, and involvement encourages wisdom. Wholeness emerges, and wholeness is oneness.

Corrie ten Boom, a Dutch woman, devoted the later years of her life to awakening people to love and forgiveness. Ms. ten Boom survived Nazi concentration camps, including Ravensbruck, the camp where her sister Betsie died. After the war, Corrie ten Boom preached "forgiving our trespassers" in over sixty countries.

In *The Hiding Place*, Ms. ten Boom shares a personal experience of forgiveness. After speaking at a church service in Germany, Ms. ten Boom recognized one of the S.S. guards from the concentration camp where she and her sister Betsie had been imprisoned and where Betsie had died. Ms. ten Boom describes what happened:

> And suddenly it was all there—the roomful of mocking men, the heaps of clothing, Betsie's pain-blanched face.
> He came up to me as the church was emptying, beaming and bowing. "How grateful I am for your message, *Fraulein*," he said. "To think that, as you say, He has washed my sins away!"
> His hand was thrust out to shake mine. And I, who had preached so often to the people in Bloemendaal the need to forgive, kept my hand at my side.
> Even as the angry, vengeful thoughts boiled through me, I saw the sin of them. Jesus Christ had died for this man; was I going to ask for more? Lord Jesus, I prayed, forgive me and help me to forgive him.
> I tried to smile, I struggled to raise my hand. I could not. I felt nothing, not the slightest spark of warmth or charity. And so again I breathed a silent prayer. Jesus, I cannot forgive him. Give me Your forgiveness.
> As I took his hand the most incredible thing happened. From my shoulder along my arm and through my hand a current seemed to pass from me to him, while into my heart sprang a love for this stranger that almost overwhelmed me.
> And so I discovered that it is not on our forgiveness any more than on our goodness that the world's healing hinges,

but on His. When he tells us to love our enemies, He gives, along with the command, the love itself.[3]

In oneness, you can come to understand that people do the best they can with the tools they have at the time. There is no right or wrong, only process. Life is journey, and you are one in journey with all people. Living this unity, forgiveness and love flow like ribbons in the wind. You know that all beings are interconnected: when you love another, you love yourself. When you forgive another, you forgive yourself. Oneness is from and of God, the wholeness of universal Good—the Good that surrounds you and resides in you.

———————

Corrie ten Boom's encounter dramatizes God's involvement in the forgiving process. Discovering her human inability to forgive, she turned to the source of all forgiveness, not because it was natural or easy, but because it was necessary. Forgiveness overthrows the enemies of the past.

Like her, you only have to be willing to forgive. At times it is difficult to be willing: you too may want to keep your hand at your side, but forgiveness *is* possible. This chapter is called "To Forgive Is to Heal," not "To Forgive Is to Like and Condone What Happened in Order to Heal." No qualifiers are imposed.

You only have to make the decision to let go, and you find comfort. A power greater than you are completes the procedure while kissing you with wisdom. When you let go, your once angry eyes can see oneness, your once angry fists can hold peace.

The act of forgiving imparts acceptance and wholeness, but the act is a choice.

———————

Chapter 14

Empowerment

Love and laughter flow in me and through me.

Take a deep breath. Hold the breath, knowing it is the spirit of eternal peace, then release it. Relax. Take a second breath. The second breath is eternal harmony. Breathe and feel union with all things. As you inhale the third breath, feel eternal love. When you exhale, visualize yourself standing in the center of a great field of wildflowers. It is a season of growth, and you stand barefoot in lush green grass. Smell the soil; dig your toes deep into the earth's richness. You are a part of the earth, one with the grassland. Allow your eyes to wander over all that surrounds you. Relax and breathe your union with all nature. Take a moment to rest in the awareness.

Stand and let the wind rock you in the universal arms of nature. You are at peace, complete. The energy of the sun seeps into the center of your being—the light of life, divine power.

Breathe deeply, in tune with all that is. At peace, experience the fullness of who you are. Mentally pick a buttercup and know you are unique and deserve respect for that uniqueness. Find a wild strawberry in the awareness that you are permitted mistakes. Hold the five-petaled forget-me-not in the joy of loving and being loved. The wild hyacinth expresses your permission to release feelings. The daisy is your right to healthy relationships. Your bouquet of wildflowers symbolizes your wholeness. You are divine goodness in union with all creation. Allow the freshness of life and the totality of earth to enter your lungs. Exhale oneness and gratitude.

A JOURNEY TO WHOLENESS

The purpose of this visualization is to help you experience your personal sense of wholeness. Through forgiveness, wholeness transforms victim into victor. The power of choice replaces futility. The process demands strength, directing you *into* rather than *away from* difficulties. "Problems," M. Scott Peck, M.D., wrote in *The Road Less Traveled*, "call forth our courage and our wisdom; indeed, they create our courage and our wisdom."[1] Adult children of alcoholics who forgive unearth both.

Wholeness sounds wonderful, and who doesn't want courage and wisdom, but when you are facing change (and recovery is change), your instinct may still be to crawl back to the familiar. I knew what life was like as a smoker: life as a nonsmoker is uncertain. Why turn to an untested Higher Power for protection when the protective powers of smoking are proven? Cigarette smoking, though dangerous, is familiar. Why change? Change is scary.

Each time I've experienced the fear of change, I've had to acknowledge that fear. For me, verbalizing the feeling puts it in perspective. And once in perspective, fear, although painful, signals progress. Trusting my Higher Power and in touch with the realization that I am getting better, I no longer have to fight. My whole being relaxes, for all is well in the moment. Through forgiveness I can go forward in peace.

But just as a college student doesn't stop by the administration hall the first week of school and pick up a bachelor's degree, an adult child of an alcoholic doesn't stop by the recovery process and pick up wellness. Healing, like a degree, takes time and work, and it demands dedication. You must commit to the requirements of your process. Once you are committed, however, there are many tools to empower recovery.

Alcoholism is often described as a physical, mental, and spiritual illness, and in reaction to the disease, adult children may have developed weaknesses in the same three areas. In the following sections, we will look at the physical, mental, and spiritual parts of ourselves and suggest some tools for healing. The divisions aren't to suggest that a person can be sliced into three neat packages; they are offered to simplify the presentation of the material. Adopt one or two of the suggestions, if you like, or devise your own techniques.

Physical

The first concern is the body. As you evolve in wholeness, honor your body through loving attention, being conscious of proper diet, regular exercise, and adequate rest.

Since I now care about my body, I take an interest in proteins, whole grains, fresh fruits and vegetables. I recognize that when I eat better, I feel better, and that when I feel better, I do better. A healthy diet is no more than a computer program for energy production. Good nutrition produces good energy.

A physically conditioned body conducts energy well. I know that, but I moan when told to exercise. My mind cannot fathom finding pleasure in any activity that produces sweat. Yet, you keep what you earn in perspiration. Statistics prove that hearty exercisers are more relaxed and more fulfilled. Exercised muscles vitalize my spirit, unexercised muscles encumber it. All the good energy released by dealing with anger and sadness may be lost in lethargy.

Getting adequate rest I'm usually good at. That's fortunate, since a good night's sleep shrinks problems and helps me stay out of extremes. Extremes are adult children's familiar playgrounds—the "verys": very angry, very sad, very grandiose, very anything. Well rested, I have a greater chance of being in balance and in charge.

Mental

Ways to work with the mental side of your nature abound like curative herbs. I've mentioned some in earlier chapters—realizing that thoughts are things, strengthening self-esteem through self-knowledge, identifying feelings.

"No secrets" is another technique I've used. "No secrets" means that someone always knows what's going on in my head, what I'm thinking, dreaming, planning. The practice encourages humility and discourages my tendency to manipulate. Telling my husband or a trusted friend what I'm up to keeps me aware of "what I'm up to" and where I'm going. An expressed thought is a manageable thought.

Many adult children find they are frightened by their own use of alcohol and prescription drugs even if they don't have chemical abuse problems. Because of the scares associated with a parent's drug misuse, these adult children feel guilty when they have a drink or take medication. "No secrets" works well here, too. Telling someone how they feel about what they're taking or drinking can lessen the problem.

The responsible use of choice is another good tool because it can counteract impulsiveness. Aware of who I am and what furthers my self-esteem, I nurture myself with wise choices. Allen, an adult child, spoke of his choice to get well: "At first I didn't like the idea of having to deal with my childhood and feelings in order to heal, and decided to forget the whole idea. Then I saw that what I was really afraid of was success. Success scared me because I wasn't used to it. Understanding that, I decided to do what had to be done. I chose wellness."

The responsible use of choice is the umbrella over all wise decisions. Allen's decision to get well is one. My decision to exercise is another. You may apply the tool to friends, career decisions, or whether or not to eat sugar cookies. You know what improves your self-esteem. Let your choices help you.

Detachment has been a powerful healing aid for me. Detachment is an ongoing learning experience that helps me separate myself from other people's actions. (It also helps me separate others from their actions.) As opposed to isolation, which involves a general disengagement from people and events, detachment is a way to live with people, yet look beyond their behaviors. It is a way to live life regardless of what another is doing. I take responsibility for my problems and don't point fingers. Cora spoke of how she detached from a brother who abused alcohol.

> My brother used to call me collect and threaten me in order to get me to send money. I couldn't love him because I was scared. Ultimately, I lost contact with him. Then last winter I travelled east and visited his last address. It turned out to be an old abandoned building. I was sick at heart and scared of the neighborhood, but I forced myself to make inquiries. Within hours my brother called me. His voice was curt, angry. I hung in with him until he finally agreed to meet me on neutral ground, a coffee shop. I decided to love my brother and to reject any of his threatening actions.
>
> We are friends now. I've chosen to separate my feelings for my brother from my feelings about what he does. If he threatens me again, I'll tell him I love him and care about him, but that I won't accept his destructive actions.

Detachment isn't easy. I slip back to old patterns like a grandmother to her memories. But knowing the importance of detachment, I try to catch myself sooner. I have learned that the best way for me to help the alcoholic in my life, or anyone else, is to take care of myself. Detaching, I let others live life as they choose, understanding that their behavior isn't intended to hurt me.

The Healing

None of this comes naturally in the beginning, but, as with exercise, you keep what you earn in perspiration. Al-Anon is a healthy place to practice these concepts and to learn new ones. Therapy can be beneficial. Go after whatever enriches your self-esteem and healing. You are worth that, and more.

Spiritual

I empower my spiritual self, the core of who I am, through prayer and meditation, going inward to commune and draw strength. Prayer and meditation are the vehicles I use to awaken answers that sleep within and around me.

Studying prayer, I learn it is seldom formal. To pray is to talk with God as I understand Him, to speak and listen with openness. Trusting the everlasting arms of God, I rest in those arms like a child, sometimes worried, sometimes joyful. All that I am I share, then I still myself and listen for direction. God's answers are simple answers: to love, to trust. In prayer, God's answers transform seeds of pain into summer lilies.

"I had the strangest experience last year," Sonia, the middle-aged daughter of an alcoholic father, said. "I'd been in a depression for a couple of months, and couldn't get out of it. Then one night when my husband and kids had gone to McDonald's to once again get supper for the family, I turned to prayer. I got on my knees and begged God for help. When I listened for His direction, I received what I thought was the most absurd message: 'Make people laugh.' At first I debated about what to do with the message. Then I decided that since nothing else had worked, I'd give laughter a try. I pinned a huge bow to the top of my head, painted my lips and cheeks bright red, and when my family returned from McDonald's, told them 'Holly Happy' had come to brighten things up. We had such fun that evening giggling and being silly. And that night, following the direction I'd received in prayer to make people laugh, my depression lifted permanently."

Meditation is similar to prayer, yet different. The goal of each is awareness, but how the goal is sought differentiates them: prayer leads to awareness through talking and listening to God, meditation through inward reflection or stillness.

Through meditation I find balance. My inner world unites with my outer world, and the realization that all is well replaces fear and anger. My energy surges. My ability to cope increases, and there is peace like spring air.

I begin by centering. Ways to do this are varied and personal. Sometimes I follow the breath at the nostrils, sometimes I count the breath (inhale-one, exhale-two, up to and including ten, and then back to one), and sometimes I use a mantra (one word repeated over and over). The purpose of centering is to clear the mind of thoughts. It's not easy. My mind tends to be a rambunctious child, so I'm forever having to guide it back to single focus. I center until I feel relaxed yet alert. This takes about fifteen minutes.

Once centered, I choose a meditation to help me shift my consciousness. Some meditations, like *creative imagination* (or guided meditation), are highly structured. Others, like *contemplation*, are unstructured. The meditation I choose will depend on which structure I'm comfortable with and what I am needing at the time: peace, unity, insight.

- *Creative imagination*, a structured meditation, is image-making. Here the conscious enters the unconscious. You used creative imagination in the room of the authentic self and, more recently, when I directed you to the field at the beginning of this chapter. Our imaginations create reality all the time. Imagining the negative can precipitate it. In meditation, you direct your imagination to achieve a reality that is positive and nurturing. Visualizing yourself as a whole person, you condition your beliefs and make yourself whole.

- With *contemplation*, an unstructured meditation, you concentrate on an item for a period of time, another fifteen minutes or so. I've used leaves or other natural things, passages from scripture, symbols from dreams. Only concentrate—a sort of staring. That's important to understand: no thinking, no intellectualizing, no commenting, no mind involvement whatsoever. Saint Theresa of Avila, when teaching contemplation to her students, wrote: "I do not require of you to form great and serious considerations in your thinking. I require of you only to look." If you *force* your mental abilities on the object, you limit what is released. Contemplation offers a "knowing" that far transcends thought by allowing the unconscious to surface into the conscious.

As a healing tool, meditation is dynamic. It is less complex than most suppose. It doesn't mean flashing visions or booming revelations. To the contrary, it is quiet self-communion that at times may even seem boring. But once I began to meditate on a regular basis, meditation altered my life. I have new energy, new understanding, new serenity. No spiritual Miracle Gro, meditation is hard work, and its gifts are unpretentious. Blessings arrive like shy guests who will feel more at home with time.

These definitions are greatly condensed and generalized. If meditation appeals to you, consult the many fine books that offer detailed studies of the art. Two I've found helpful are *How to Meditate: A Guide to Self-Discovery*, by

Lawrence LeShan, and *Meditation: Commonsense Directions for an Uncommon Life*, by Eknath Easwaran. When you study this healing art, you'll discover that a variety of techniques exist. Test a number of them, then isolate your favorites and design a meditation program to meet your needs.

Prayer and meditation, in combination with physical and mental awareness, empower your wholeness. And approaching wholeness you discover

> There is peace
> harmony
> love
> right thought
> right action
> in this whole situation.
> —Anonymous

And in all situations. Approaching wholeness, I find that life has new meaning. I have walked into my past and claimed my wound. I claim my wound not to replay or rebury it, but so that I can lay it open to the light of healing.

Sister Virginia Mary Barta, O.S.F., the director of the retreat center I often visit, once said this to me: "Put your wound forward, Patty. Imagine it is a disfigured foot. Though your instinct may be to hide the foot behind the normal one, don't. If you do, you will fall. Place the foot out in front and stand on it, and you will not only stand straight, you will grow stronger by allowing other people to see the wound and identify with it."

From Sister Virginia I have learned I can do more because of where I have been. My wound becomes, in her words, my "divine" wound, my gift.

EXERCISE #41

The Healing Light

In a spirit of closure and commencement, I invite you to know your gift through "The Healing Light," a meditation that embodies protection, forgiveness, recovery, wholeness. This final exercise in the workbook celebrates your journey home. Standing straight.

1. Begin to center. Take a deep breath, then exhale slowly. Dismissing all thoughts from your mind, concentrate on the breath at the nostrils. Feel the cool air as you inhale, the warm air as you exhale. Continue to follow the breath as you relax. If your mind wanders, gently bring it back to the task. Follow the breath. Relax.

2. When you are ready, visualize yourself standing healed and radiant. You are an adult child of an alcoholic who is working hard to find balance. Today you are complete and whole. Notice your peaceful spirit, your quiet breath, your relaxed muscles. In time you become aware that there is a gold and white light above your head. Experience the power in the light, then watch as it gradually becomes a waterfall of light coating your body. Feel its warmth on your face and neck. Feel it cover your arms and chest. The light pours over your abdomen, your legs, your feet. As your body absorbs the warmth of the light, you realize that the waterfall has become a bubble to protect you. Breathe deeply and notice that any unpleasant feelings you might have had have been washed away in the light. You are happy and free from suffering. You are whole. You are integrating where you have been with reality. The healing light protects you. Stay in the pleasurable feelings as long as you'd like.

3. When you wish to go on, visualize someone you love very much. Bring him or her into the protected bubble with you. Allow the healing light to surround you both. Wish the person happiness, freedom from suffering, patience and warmth. Then in fullness and completion, lovingly let the person walk from the bubble.

4. Next, remembering that you are in a protected bubble where nothing can harm you, visualize someone you'd like to forgive. Slowly bring that person into the warmth of the healing bubble. Allow the gold and white light to envelop you both. Then, wishing goodwill for the person and wanting him or her to be free from suffering, permit the person to walk out of the bubble.

5. Once again you are alone in the light. Notice that you are radiating goodness and gratitude. You are one with the universe, loving and being loved. You may wish to bring in your bouquet of wildflowers or perhaps an item from the room of your authentic self as a symbol of the awareness. Whatever you choose to do, from this time forward you possess a deep knowing that you are complete, and that everything you need is already contained within you. You are in touch with your center of truth. Breathe deeply of the experience and stay in the warmth as long as you'd like. When you return to your everyday environment, you will be refreshed and alert.

―――――――――

As the book comes to an end, be proud of yourself and the fine work you are doing. Stand in the freedom and peace you have earned. You have chosen to make changes in your life and, listening to your truth center, you are implementing those changes by perceiving things in a new way and making new decisions. Being a child of an alcoholic has meant being an individual in extremes—"too much" or "too little." That can end now.

Announce your power. Living your decisions permits you, not the shadows of the past, to be in charge of your life. You are claiming your dignity, your inherent right to be who you are.

"It is the spirit in man, the breath of the Almighty, that makes him understand" (Job 32:8). You have honored that spirit. In humanity and oneness you have chosen to understand that you are more because of where you have been. Welcome home. May the breath of the Almighty continue to empower you.

Acknowledgments

Many people have given generous amounts of their time and souls to the writing of this book. Their insights bathe the work, and I am indebted.

A special thank-you to Mary Anne Scherman, M.S.W., M. Ed., an early believer who guided and affirmed me from the initial outline to the final draft. Her suggestions were crucial; her feedback, precise. I'm most grateful to Ms. Scherman for proposing many of the exercises in chapter 3, and for providing 90 percent of the information in chapter 10.

I want to thank Raymond Mosko, Ph.D. Some people's kindness is beyond words. Dr. Mosko's recommendations were always followed by a statement to suggest that he was learning as he assisted me. I learned from his humility.

A warm thank-you, also, to my dear friend Eric. Week upon week Eric read the manuscript from the viewpoint of an adult child. And week upon week my friend enriched the task with comments such as, "Watch out here, Patty, you let me speed-read. You better be more specific." Or, "Oh yes. That happened at my house too, but I think you spell commitment with only one *t*." Invaluable.

And to Edith Peterson, M.S.T., my deepest thanks and appreciation. Edith's editorial skills and keen sense of human nature strengthen each chapter. As a teacher, co-leader of a support group, and an advanced transactional analysis pupil who studied under Mary and Bob Golding, Ms. Peterson's suggestions bubbled from various broths. She made me question and rethink and feed many a spindly concept and sentence.

Without Sister Virginia Mary Barta, O.S.F., and the other core members of the Christine Center for Meditation, I'm convinced this book would not have been born. With her guidance, and because of the Center's hospitality, I've been able to find the stillness that is enabling my own healing. Sister's gentle directions encourage my journey; her "all is well" and "good news, bad news—who knows?" can encourage the reader's.

My sisters deserve my heart's thanks. How very much I love them. How proud I am of their courage. Their unceasing support and unfailing hope were my mainstay as I wrote this book. Our mutual cry is that someday our mother will be well.

I also love, and thank, the hundreds of adult children who unselfishly examined old wounds for the quotations you find in the work. "If this helps one person, I'll be happy," I heard again and again. All of the adult children's names have been changed in the book, but none of their fervor.

Notes

Preface

1. Joseph Goldstein, *The Experience of Insight: A Simple and Direct Guide to Buddhist Meditation* (Boulder: Shambhala, 1983), 20-21.

Chapter 1

1. Adapted from "Mind Room," by Marianne Andersen and Louis Savary, *Passages: A Guide to Pilgrims of the Mind* (New York: Harper & Row, 1972), 82.

2. Allen E. Wiesen, *Positive Therapy: Making The Best of Everything* (Chicago: Nelson-Hall, 1977), 60.

3. Wiesen, *Positive Therapy: Making the Best of Everything*, 67.

Chapter 2

1. W. Hugh Missildine, *Your Inner Child of the Past* (New York: Simon and Schuster, 1982), 27.

2. Missildine, *Your Inner Child of the Past*, 27.

Chapter 5

1. Sharon Wegscheider, *The Family Trap: No One Escapes from a Chemically Dependent Family* (St. Paul: Nurturing Networks, 1976).

Chapter 7

1. Missildine, *Your Inner Child of the Past*, 14.

2. Claudia Black, *It Will Never Happen to Me!* (Denver: M.A.C., 1981), 136.

Chapter 8

1. Joseph Campbell, ed., trans. by R.F.C. Hull, *The Portable Jung* (New York: Viking Press, 1971), 9.

2. *The Portable Jung*, 11.

3. Thomas Merton, *The Way of Chuang Tzu* (New York: New Directions, 1965), 112.

4. Dag Hammarskjöld, *Markings* (New York: Alfred A. Knopf, 1964), 13.

Chapter 9

1. Dennis L. Breo, "Ex-first lady's struggle with alcohol symbolic," *American Medical News* 28, no. 10 (March 1985), 2.

2. Breo, 2.

Chapter 10

1. Thomas Merton, *Thoughts in Solitude* (New York: Farrar, Straus and Giroux, 1983), 56.

Chapter 11

1. Ken Keyes, Jr., *Handbook to Higher Consciousness*, 5th ed. (Coos Bay, Oreg.: Living Love, 1975), 153.

2. Thomas Berry, "Our Children: Their Future," *the little magazine* 1, no. 10 (October 1982): 9.

Chapter 12

1. Merton, *The Way of Chuang Tzu*, 155.

Chapter 13

1. Adapted from: Emmet Fox, *Power Through Constructive Thinking* (New York: Harper & Row, 1932), 38.

2. Gerald G. Jampolsky, *Love Is Letting Go of Fear* (Millbrae, Calif.: Celestial Arts, 1979), 66.

3. Corrie ten Boom, with John Sherrill and Elizabeth Sherrill, *The Hiding Place* (Old Tappan, N.J.: Fleming H. Revell, 1971), 238.

Chapter 14

1. M. Scott Peck, *The Road Less Traveled: A New Psychology of Love, Traditional Values and Spiritual Growth* (New York: Simon and Schuster, 1978), 16.

Resources

Al-Anon. *One Day at a Time in Al-Anon.* New York: Al-Anon Family Group Headquarters, 1984.

Allen, James. *As a Man Thinketh.* Mount Vernon, N.Y.: The Peter Pauper Press, N.d.

Andersen, Marianne, and Louis Savary. *Passages: A Guide to Pilgrims of The Mind.* New York: Harper & Row, 1972.

Berry, Thomas. "Our Children: Their Future." *the little magazine* 1, no. 10 (October 1982): 9.

Black, Claudia. *It Will Never Happen to Me!* Denver: M.A.C., 1981.

Breo, Dennis L. "Ex-first lady's struggle with alcohol symbolic." *American Medical News* 28, no. 10 (March 1985).

Campbell, Joseph, ed. Trans. by R. F. C. Hull. *The Portable Jung.* New York: Viking Press, 1971.

Capacchione, Lucia. *The Creative Journal: The Art of Finding Yourself.* Athens, Ohio: Swallow Press, 1979.

Carnes, Patrick J. *Understanding Us.* Minneapolis: Interpersonal Communications Programs, 1981.

Davidson, Glen W. *Understanding Mourning: A Guide for Those Who Grieve.* Minneapolis: Augsburg, 1984.

de Mello, Anthony. *The Song of the Bird.* Chicago: Loyola University Press, 1982.

Donnelly, Doris. *Learning to Forgive.* New York: Macmillan, 1982.

Easwaran, Eknath. *Meditation: Commonsense Directions for an Uncommon Life.* Petaluma, Calif.: Nilgiri Press, 1978.

Ellison, Craig W. *Saying Good-bye to Loneliness and Finding Intimacy.* New York: Harper & Row, 1983.

Forman, Keith, and Walt Schafer. *Stress, Distress, and Growth.* Davis, Calif.: Responsible Action, 1978.

Fox, Emmet. *Power Through Constructive Thinking.* New York: Harper & Row, 1932.

Fox, Matthew. *Original Blessing.* Santa Fe: Bear & Company, 1983.

Garfield, Patricia. *Creative Dreaming.* New York: Ballantine, 1974.

Goldstein, Joseph. *The Experience of Insight: A Simple and Direct Guide to Buddhist Meditation.* Boulder: Shambhala, 1983.

Hammarskjöld, Dag. *Markings.* New York: Alfred A. Knopf, 1964.

Hayes, Robert J., and Richard J. Payne. *Discovery in Prayer.* New York: Paulist Press, 1969.

Hays, Edward. *Pray All Ways.* Easton, Kans.: Forest of Peace Books, 1981.

Jampolsky, Gerald G. *Love Is Letting Go of Fear.* Millbrae, Calif.: Celestial Arts, 1979.

Jensen, Amy Hillyard. *Healing Grief.* Redmond, Wash.: Medic Publishing, 1980.

Jongeward, Dorothy, and Muriel James. *Winning with People.* Reading, Mass.: Addison-Wesley, 1973.

Jung, C. G. *Memories, Dreams, Reflections.* Trans. by Richard Winston and Clara Winston, and edited by Aniela Jaffe. New York: Vintage Books, 1965.

Kellerman, Joseph. *Alcoholism: A Merry-Go-Round Named Denial.* Minneapolis: Hazelden, 1980.

Keyes, Ken, Jr. *Handbook to Higher Consciousness.* 5th ed. Coos Bay, Oreg.: Living Love, 1975.

Larsen, Earnie. *For Adult Children of Alcoholics and Those Who Love Them.* Brooklyn Park, Minn.: E. Larsen Enterprises, 1984. Audiocassette.

Leban, Adrienne. *Inner Energy.* Brookline, Mass.: Autumn Press, 1979.

Leite, Evelyn. *Detachment: The Art of Letting Go While Living with an Alcoholic.* Minneapolis: Johnson Institute, 1980.

Leonard, Linda Schierse. *The Wounded Woman: Healing the Father-Daughter Relationship.* Boulder: Shambhala, 1983.

LeShan, Lawrence. *How to Meditate: A Guide to Self-Discovery.* Boston: Little, Brown & Co., 1975.

Linn, Dennis, and Matthew Linn. *Healing Life's Hurts.* New York: Paulist Press, 1978.

Merton, Thomas. *Thoughts in Solitude.* New York: Farrar, Straus and Giroux, 1983.

————. *The Way of Chuang Tzu.* New York: New Directions, 1965.

————. *Zen and the Birds of Appetite.* New York: New Directions, 1968.

Miller, Sherod, Elam W. Nunnally, and Daniel B. Wackman, with Roger H. Ferris. *Couple Workbook: Increasing Awareness and Communication Skills.* Minneapolis: Interpersonal Communications Program, 1976.

Missildine, W. Hugh. *Your Inner Child of the Past.* New York: Simon and Schuster, 1982.

Peck, M. Scott. *The Road Less Traveled: A New Psychology of Love, Traditional Values and Spiritual Growth.* New York: Simon and Schuster, 1978.

Rama, Swami. *A Practical Guide to Holistic Healing.* Honesdale, Pa.: Himalayan International Institute, 1978.

Rozman, Deborah. *Meditating with Children.* Boulder Creek, Colo.: University of the Trees Press, 1975.

Rubin, Theodore Isaac. *The Angry Book.* New York: Macmillan, 1970.

Sanford, John A. *Healing and Wholeness.* New York: Paulist Press, 1977.

Schmelig, Randolph and Leddy. *Patterns for Self-unfoldment.* Unity Village, Mo.: Unity Books, 1975.

Seixas, Judith S., and Geraldine Youcha. *Children of Alcoholism: A Survivor's Manual.* New York: Crown, 1985.

Simon, Nissa. "How Drinking Affects the Family," *Parents Magazine* 59, no. 10 (October 1984).

ten Boom, Corrie, with John Sherrill and Elizabeth Sherrill. *The Hiding Place.* Old Tappan, N.J.: Fleming H. Revell, 1971.

Viscott, Daniel. *The Language of Feelings.* New York: Simon and Schuster, 1977.

Walters, Richard P. *Anger: Yours & Mine & What to Do About It.* Grand Rapids, Mich.: Zondervan, 1981.

Wanderer, Dr. Zev, and Tracy Cabot. *Letting Go: A 12-Week Personal Action Program to Overcome a Broken Heart.* New York: Warner Books, 1979.

Wegscheider, Sharon. *The Family Trap: No One Escapes from a Chemically Dependent Family.* St. Paul: Nurturing Networks, 1976.

Wiesen, Allen E. *Positive Therapy: Making the Best of Everything.* Chicago: Nelson-Hall, 1977.

Woititz, Janet Geringer. *Adult Children of Alcoholics.* Hollywood, Fla.: Health Communications, 1983.